D0437914

Stonehenge of the Kings

BY THE SAME AUTHOR

The Prehistoric Ridge Way: A Journey

1. Part of regalia buried with a tall, well-built man under Bush Barrow near Stonehenge, including gold breastplate, a thirteen-inch-long dagger, a smaller dagger (the haft of which was decorated with thousands of gold pins), and a sceptre. A royal burial at the Stonehenge capital.

STONEHENGE OF THE KINGS

A People Appear

PATRICK CRAMPTON

THE JOHN DAY COMPANY
NEW YORK

FIRST AMERICAN EDITION 1968

Library of Congress Catalogue
Card Number: 68-24144

PRINTED IN THE UNITED STATES OF AMERICA

Contents

	INTRODUCTION	*page* 1
1	Mount Prescelly	3
2	Stonehenge and Mycenae	9
3	Indo-European Myth	17
4	Sky God and Great Goddess	27
5	The Second 'City'	34
6	Religion from the Mediterranean	45
7	The Wessex Culture	55
8	The Five 'Cities' of Stonehenge Wessex	62
9	Revelation at Clickhimin	70
10	The Irish Myths	82
11	Tara of the Kings	95
12	The Fifth 'City' and the Road to Stonehenge	101
13	The 'Stonehenge Language'	110
14	Sea Trade	119
15	Controversy and Stonehenge the Building	130
16	Temple – or Home?	140
17	The New Concept	158
	SELECT BIBLIOGRAPHY	167
	INDEX	169

Illustrations

I	Bush Barrow grave goods	*frontispiece*
II	Stonehenge	*following page* 80
III	The henge at Avebury	
IV	New Grange roof	
V	Megalithic Art at New Grange	
VI	Winterbourne Stoke Barrow Group	
VII	Gold breastplate from Clandon barrow	
VIII	Upton Lovell necklace	
IX	Sceptre-head from Clandon Barrow	
X	Little Woodbury	
XI	King's Quarters at Clickhimin	
XII	The broch at Mousa, Shetland Isles	
XIII	Clickhimin	
XIV	Emain Macha	
XV	Lambourn Seven Barrows	
XVI	'Tara of the Kings'	
XVII	The Rillaton gold cup	
XVIII	Gold from Wessex Barrows	
XIX	Bronze Age ship	
XX	Golden Barrow grave goods	
XXI	Scandinavian ship-carvings	
XXII	Stanton Harcourt	
XXIII	Plan of Woodhenge and an Iron Age house	
XXIV	A reconstruction of Woodhenge	
XXV	Bronze Age battle axes	
XXVI	The henge at Arminghall	
XXVII	Aerial photograph of Woodhenge	
XXVIII	'Circles' at Highworth	

ILLUSTRATIONS

Drawings in Text

	Distribution map of Wessex	xii–xiii
Fig. A	Concentration of ruins around Stonehenge	29
Fig. B	The Dorset Cursus	66
Fig. C	Evolution of forts	76
Fig. D	Detail of North Ferriby ship	127
Fig. E	Post circles under barrows	150
Fig. F	Plans of Sanctuary and Iron Age houses	151

Acknowledgements

I wish to express my thanks to a number of people and organisations who kindly supplied me with material to illustrate this book. They are as follows:

J. F. S. Stone and Thames and Hudson Ltd for permission to include Fig. A; L. V. Grinsell and Methuen Ltd who permitted me to use the Wessex distribution map which appears on the end-papers; Stuart Piggott and Edinburgh University Press who supplied Fig. F (Iron Age House Plans), and Associated Book Publishers Ltd for permission to include Fig. B.

I am indebted to Peter Rawstorne for Plates IV and V; to J. K. St. Joseph for Plates XIV and XVI; to Stanley Thomas for Plate XVII; to Dennis Harding and Ian M. Blake for Plate XXIII (Iron Age House) and to Paul Ashbee for Fig. E.

My thanks are also due to Universsitetets Oldsaksamling, Oslo, who supplied Plate XXI; to E. V. Wright and the Prehistoric Society for Fig. D; to the National Maritime Museum for Plate XIX; to Stanley Thomas and Devizes Museum for Plates I, VIII, XVIII, XX and XXV, and to the Ashmolean Museum, Oxford, for Plates III, VI, XV, XXII and XXVIII.

Plates II, X, XI, XII, XIII, XXIII (Plan of Woodhenge), XXVI and XXVII and Figs. C and F are Crown Copyright.

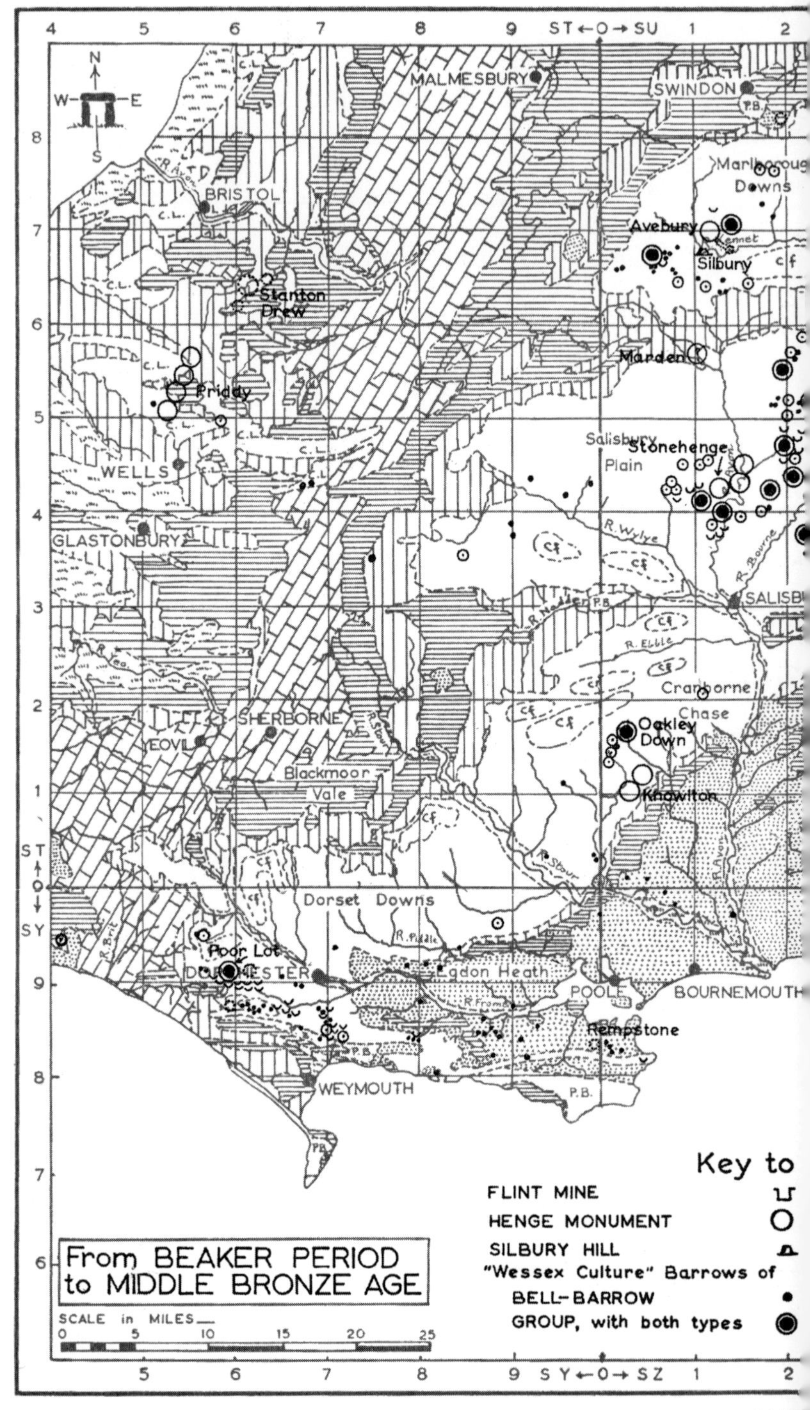
N
S
W
E
ST←O→SU
SY←O→SZ
MALMESBURY
SWINDON
P.B.
Downs
BRISTOL
C.L.
R. Avon
Avebury
Kennet
Silbury
Stanton
Drew
Marden
Priddy
WELLS
Salisbury
Plain
Stonehenge
GLASTONBURY
R. Wylye
R. Bourne
R. Nadder
R. Ebble
Cranborne
Chase
SHERBORNE
YEOVIL
R. Stour
Blackmoor
Vale
Oakley
Down
Knowlton
Dorset Downs
R. Piddle
Poor Lot
DORCHESTER
Egdon Heath
R. Frome
POOLE
BOURNEMOUTH
Rempstone
WEYMOUTH
From BEAKER PERIOD
to MIDDLE BRONZE AGE
SCALE in MILES
0 5 10 15 20 25
Key to
FLINT MINE
HENGE MONUMENT
SILBURY HILL
"Wessex Culture" Barrows of
BELL-BARROW
GROUP, with both types

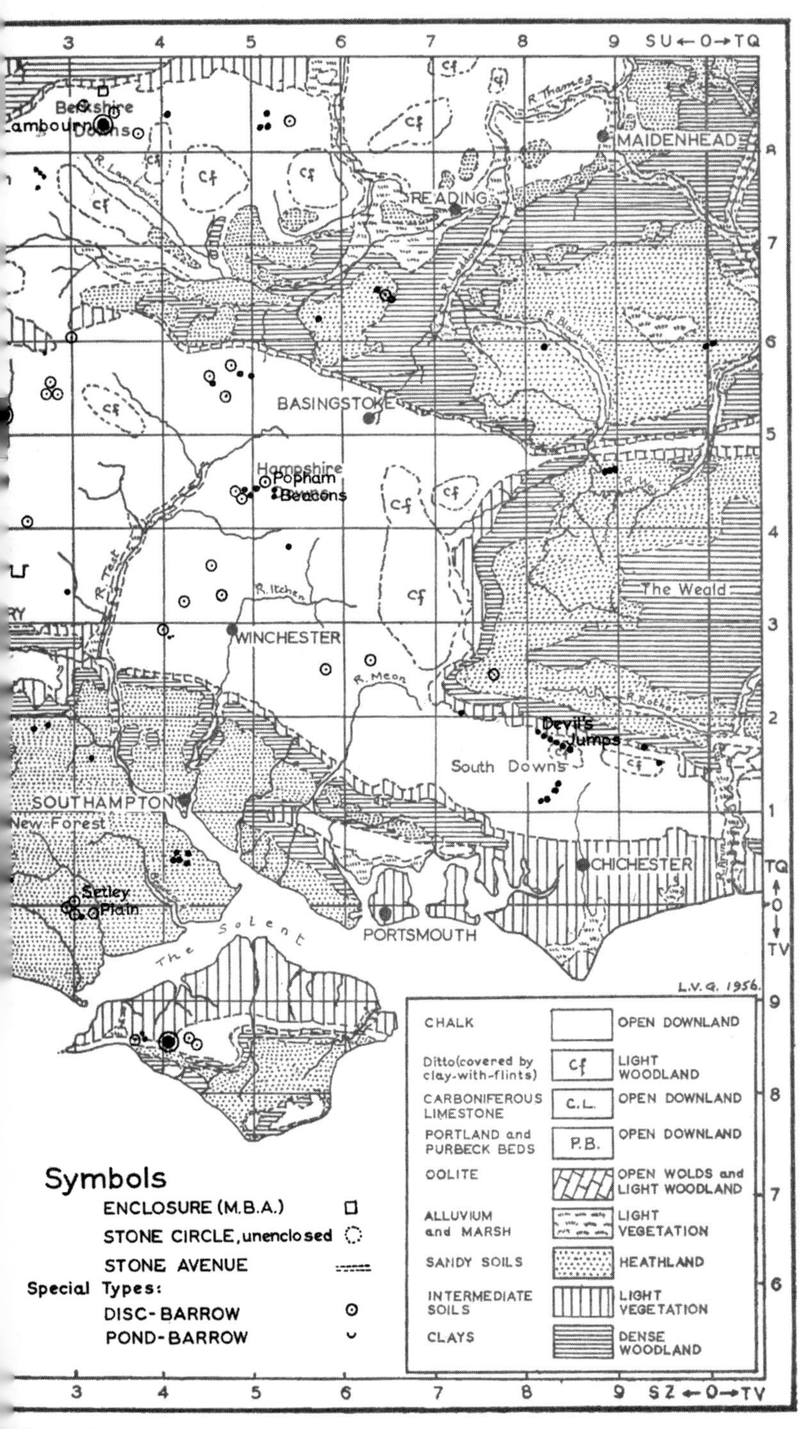
Berkshire Downs
Lambourn
MAIDENHEAD
READING
R. Thames
R. Lambourn
R. Blackwater
BASINGSTOKE
Hampshire Downs
Popham Beacons
R. Wey
R. Test
R. Itchen
The Weald
WINCHESTER
R. Meon
R. Rother
Devil's Jumps
South Downs
SOUTHAMPTON
New Forest
CHICHESTER
Setley Plain
The Solent
PORTSMOUTH
L.V.G. 1956.
SU ← 0 → TQ
SZ ← 0 → TV
Symbols
ENCLOSURE (M.B.A.)
STONE CIRCLE, unenclosed
STONE AVENUE
Special Types:
DISC-BARROW
POND-BARROW
CHALK — OPEN DOWNLAND
Ditto (covered by clay-with-flints) — Cf — LIGHT WOODLAND
CARBONIFEROUS LIMESTONE — C.L. — OPEN DOWNLAND
PORTLAND and PURBECK BEDS — P.B. — OPEN DOWNLAND
OOLITE — OPEN WOLDS and LIGHT WOODLAND
ALLUVIUM and MARSH — LIGHT VEGETATION
SANDY SOILS — HEATHLAND
INTERMEDIATE SOILS — LIGHT VEGETATION
CLAYS — DENSE WOODLAND

VERLAP

Stonehenge of the Kings

Introduction

I started to write this book to present the great mass of fact that was known about Stonehenge Britain. Approximate dates were known; magnificent adornment; surprising architectural evidence, for that time; fine pottery styles; efficient weapons.

The evidence had suggested that Stonehenge society was 'heroic'; that is, similar to society in Homer's *Iliad* – ruled by a king, with a warrior aristocracy, and a mass of commoners and bondspeople. Through archaeology, a number of cultures had emerged and these could be associated with individual structural monuments, such as Woodhenge and Stonehenge. An enormous, amorphous collection of details about Stonehenge Britain existed.

This was the situation while I wrote the first eight chapters of the book. The Ordnance Survey had stated the position regarding Stonehenge society in *Field Archaeology*, published in 1963, '. . . we have no real idea of precisely where and how they lived.'

Archaeology is a branch of historical research studying people through remains, and without this knowledge of where and how they lived, the goal could not be seen; the societies of Stonehenge Britain lay undiscovered; the people that once existed could be seen as individuals through their skeletal remains and grave-goods, but not collectively as motivated societies; there was knowledge of detail but no understanding.

Two things became stressed in my mind; the first, the importance of the 'heroic' evidence, the kingly and warrior burials, with the frequent occurrence of weapons; the second, that the third–second millennia ruins in Wessex were arranged in five concentrated groups at Lambourn, Avebury, Stonehenge, Oakley-Knowlton, and Dorchester, Dorset. Each of these groups had been dissected by archaeology, the primary evidence of Woodhenge, say, dating it to 2000 BC and that of nearby, architectural Stonehenge to 1500 BC, thus dissociating the two. It seemed essential to me, that, the detailed knowledge of individual monuments having been gained, the overriding significance of these five areas of ruins should be restated, as revealing evidence of continuing barbarian social life through many centuries.

The catalyst to the amorphous ingredients of what was known of barbarian life in Britain came with the excavation of a fort at Clickhimin in the Shetland Isles by Mr J. R. C. Hamilton, Inspector of Ancient Monuments, Ministry of Public Building and Works. He wrote in 1965, 'For the first time, the domestic arrangements inside an early Celtic fortress were completely revealed.' With this knowledge, barbarian social life was understood, and the ancient epic material of Ireland and classical writings, at last, shed a brilliant light on barbarian archaeology. The social life conclusively revealed was quite different from that previously interpreted from archaeology alone; different and socially up-graded. For instance, people were living upstairs in tribal forts, and not scattered over the countryside in huts. At Clickhimin, a discovery of the most supreme historic importance had been made.

After Chapter 8, the book associates these three factors: (1) heroic societies, (2) the five groups of ruins, (3) the evidence of Clickhimin. From this association a social picture of the Stonehenge people emerges. I do not claim this picture to be absolute truth, but I do consider that elements of it are so consistent, one with another, that at last Stonehenge society can be seen as people, and not as mysterious wraiths congregating to build temples and bury their dead and then vanishing away into the mists; wraiths with little thought other than religion and the ritual of death, or, as has been put forward recently, a preoccupation with advanced astronomy.

Through misinterpretation, the concept of Stonehenge society was puzzlingly anomalous – warrior, yet with no defence structures; talented, yet with no homes. After Clickhimin, these anomalies no longer exist. The concept coalesces; we begin to understand.

I am grateful to Mr Paul Ashbee for reading and criticising the manuscript, to Mr J. R. C. Hamilton for reading and commenting on it, to Dr H. B. Trumper for criticising the first two chapters and to Dr I. F. Smith for commenting on Chapter 5. Professor R. J. C. Atkinson kindly supplied me with information on a number of specific points. In no case are they responsible for what I have written.

P.C.

CHAPTER I

Mount Prescelly

'. . . *all-seeing Zeus sitting on the topmost of Olympus' many peaks.*' THE ILIAD[1]

I WAS standing on Mount Prescelly in south-west Wales. I had driven alone that morning from my cottage in the Black Mountains, seventy miles to the east. It had seemed a long drive, sweeping down the windings of river- and stream-cut valleys, with the roadmen's long-handled shovels witnessing that I was far nearer to Ireland than to London. Looking back now over my route from the top of Prescelly, the mountains of south Wales receded grey-blue into the distance. As far again, beyond my Black Mountains, from which I had come with little more effort than the slightest pressure of my right foot, a ceremonial building of unique and massive structure, in itself symbolising an astonishing wealth and power in its builders, lifts its stones from the turf of Salisbury Plain. We now call this building Stonehenge. The name its own peoples gave it is unknown.

Some of these peoples, not very long after 2000 BC, had a compulsion to transport at least eighty stones, weighing up to four tons apiece, from the exact area of mountain top on which I was standing to Salisbury Plain – a distance of one hundred and thirty-five miles as the crow flies. There the stones were used in the complex design of Stonehenge, and later arranged in the great stone building of more local sarsen stone.

These peoples; the beliefs they held; the centuries of the power of the bluestones from Prescelly, until the final architectural splendour of Stonehenge was built; it is these things this book is about – the record of a journey of research and physical exploration, the fascination of which never failed or fails in drawing me on. So much of early barbarian Britain unfolds on this journey with major arrival points but no final end.

I turned on the crag of bluestone to face the rushing wind, and looked westward. The valley of the River Nevern ran from me to make a shallow V eight miles off, partially framing a foreground of grey, silver and pale blue sea, which swept out to the horizon. Above, cumulus clouds sailed towards me in a cobalt sky, sailing from Ireland to Wales, just as the ships of the merchants with their gold, copper and valuable stone did when all roads, particularly that from Ireland, were drawn to the wealth of Stonehenge.

I strained my eyes over the sea on this fine April day, but Ireland, seventy miles away, was not visible to me, although I was looking from a height of 1,195 feet. How thankful the seamen must have been in bad weather to recognise the unmistakable shapes of the outcrops of bluestone on Mount Prescelly. The other mountains about stood smooth-domed. Only eastern Prescelly had these pinnacles of stone, like Dartmoor tors, but upturned in their grain, so that rock-faces rose vertically in irregular, cubistic and trianguloid columns sometimes forty feet above the smooth, sheep-bitten turf and April-brown heather.

Mount Prescelly clearly had particular significance to Neolithic and Bronze Age man. The widespread concept of gods living on mountains was a natural one. To the Greeks, Mount Olympus was the home of Zeus from antiquity into historic times, and this is how I regard Mount Prescelly, following such authorities as Sir Cyril Fox and Professor R. J. C. Atkinson.

I, myself, a man of this scientific age, found it strangely impressive in its form, setting, and utter loneliness as I picked my way through peat-bog and over heather across the mile-long saddle between Carn Meini and Foel Trigarn, the bluestone outcrops at either end. A fine fox, with heavy coat, gleaming ruddy and sable, whisked out of the heather a few yards ahead of me, and loped over the brow, downhill. Curlews called at times. Otherwise Prescelly was reserved to me and its god.

The god had no direct effect on me. He was dead, like Zeus. In any case, I am not susceptible to the occult. But my senses were responsive to this long-awaited visit, and through Bronze Age eyes I could see the god – like a sick child in the pattern of its bedroom wallpaper – in the shape of a cloud and among the rocks.

I was the only man on Mount Prescelly. Even below, in the valley to the east, small white buildings showed pathetically spaced over the vast slope of down-curving mountain to the peat-bog in its floor; strikingly similar in its brown and green tones and sparseness of humanity to western Ireland. To my right now, half-way over the saddle, I saw a familiar curve and turned to examine Carn Ferched, a turf-covered, round, burial cairn. This would be of the times of the bluestones, and as the lone man-made structure on the saddle between the outcrops, its isolation seemed to make it significant. But this is not matched by its size, just over a foot high and eighteen paces across – a pale shadow of the huge bell and bowl barrows around Stonehenge. No king was buried here – though the power of kings is not always measured by the size of a burial mound.

The rucksack was heavy on my back with fragments of stone from Carn Meini. Many had shown a uniform, crystal-winking blue surface when I fractured them. Geologists call this rock unspotted dolerite. The name 'bluestone' is not fanciful. One is used to grey or buff stone but the blue colour of this stone is arresting. Other stones I broke had a similar surface, but spaced over the blue were pea-sized cream-coloured spots of felspar. This variety is called spotted dolerite. There are also other geological varieties of bluestone at Stonehenge, but Mount Prescelly is the source of them all. These rocks do not outcrop anywhere except in the square mile between Carn Meini and Foel Trigarn. As I reached the screes at the foot of Foel Trigarn, I added more fragments of bluestone to my collection.

There was something akin to magic when I cracked a stone on a remote, particular hill in the far west of Wales, and a distinctive mottled surface appeared that was so familiar to me at distant Stonehenge. I found it satisfying to be looking at the evidence in my own hand of one of the greatest feats ever accomplished by a barbarian people anywhere in the world.

The outcrops of Foel Trigarn are like buttresses against its sides rather than crowns on its peak, unlike Carn Meini at the far end of the saddle, and its top is surmounted by a hill-fort of an age when man had found iron and this god of Bronze Age Britain had been overcome by gods and goddesses of war and fertility, of whom we know many things from the Celtic myths and archaeology. The earlier conceptions of some of these Celtic deities, particularly the goddesses, lie far back, it may be beyond, even, the days of the bluestones.

I toiled up the steep-rising face of Foel Trigarn between the buttresses of bluestone, and on the leeward side of one I found a natural seat in the rock. I smoked a pipe in still air, except for an occasional eddy, while the wind from Ireland roared round the crag with the noise of an express train. No Bronze Age shipmaster would have put to sea in a wind like this. The omens of gods and weather had to be favourable for open sea voyages, experienced seamen though they were.

Jason, the Bronze Age voyager for the Golden Fleece, when storm-bound at the foot of the mountain called Dindymum, is advised by Mopsus, the seer of the Argonauts, 'My lord, you must climb this holy peak to propitiate Rhea, Mother of all the happy gods, whose lovely throne is Dindymum itself – and then the gales will cease.' When the Argonauts had assembled on top of Dindymum, 'Jason, pouring libations on the blazing sacrifice, earnestly besought the goddess to send the stormy winds elsewhere.'[2]

The living picture that is created by substituting 'Prescelly' for 'Dindymum' in this passage is what inspires me to write this book. The words are people speaking, and it is this that is so difficult to catch as you stand silent in Stonehenge.

Could there be any more specific reason for this substitution, other than the two peaks being holy, and the mere wish to visualise living people in Stonehenge Britain? I think there is. I believe, and it is one of the themes of this book, that a Greek adventurer, similar to Jason, was in Britain at the time of the building of Stonehenge.

I tapped my pipe out on a bluestone, a mildly disturbing sense of desecration crossing my mind as the ash fell on it. Going up into the hill-fort of Foel Trigarn, I found the three great cairns it encloses. Built of boulders and nodules, mostly of a size for one man to carry, these stand unclothed with turf on the peak of Foel Trigarn. From my own height, I estimated the largest to be ten feet high. But for the difference in the stone, I could have been looking at one of the groups of cairns on the crests of Dartmoor.

My first visit to Prescelly was coming to a close. I had explored the peak. There had been no positive sign of past quarrying for the bluestones. After the weathering of nearly four thousand years, the traces of the detachment by man of these columnar stones would disappear. The loose screes below, in any case, could still supply innumerable bluestones to match the shape of those at Stonehenge, so possibly the source of the sacred stones was there. Except for the hill-fort of Prescelly, which was irrelevant to Stonehenge, because of its late prehistoric date, only Carn Ferched and the three cairns on Foel Trigarn showed the activity of man. One would expect to find no more on a holy mountain.

I looked back from the rampart of the hill-fort towards Carn Meini, the smaller outcrops curving away from me, and beyond the ridge continuing upward to the smooth line of Prescelly Top, the highest peak of south-west Wales.

Southward from where I stood, began the route that Professor Atkinson thinks was that over which the bluestones were taken to Stonehenge. This starts with an overland journey of sixteen miles to Milford Haven. Here the Altar Stone of Stonehenge, which is of a sandstone outcropping at Milford Haven, was added to the bluestones. The stones were then transported by sea up the Bristol Channel, and then on river-craft along the Bristol Avon. Branching from this river up its tributary the River Frome would take the stones by water as far as where the town of Frome now is. A land haul of six miles would take them to the River Wylie. A boulder of bluestone has been found in Boles Barrow, a Neolithic long barrow situated near the River Wylie. The River Wylie joins the Salisbury Avon which would carry them to within two miles of Stonehenge. All that remained was their hauling in triumphal procession up the Stonehenge Avenue to the temple itself.

A stupendous feat. And yet, perhaps, not quite so astonishing when one considers that it was carried out by what was rapidly developing into a highly organised society, whose wealth was so great that even Mycenae, 'rich in gold', in Mediterranean Europe was aware of it; a wealth that could afford to build Avebury, the largest ceremonial structure in Europe; that could afford the tremendous expense of Stonehenge, the only architect-designed building in northern Europe; a wealth created by handling most of the alluvial gold that left Ireland, the treasure-house of north-west Europe. We shall see the evidence that it was a society ruled by a king, whose power extended over much of Britain, and whose trading links spread to Ireland, Scandinavia, Central Europe, Brittany, Crete and Mycenae.

Until comparatively recently this society of Stonehenge, reminiscent in some ways of that of the Greek heroes with which it was in general contemporary, was unknown and unsuspected. In fact, one still sees misleading pictures of the sophisticated curves and perspectives of Stonehenge with aboriginal-like humans in crude skins squatting in the foreground. Nothing could be further from the truth of this zenith of prehistoric Britain – a lost chapter which is being excitingly pieced together.

I dropped straight downhill to the road set on the side of the valley which looked like a bit of western Ireland. As I walked along the road, with the weight of the holy stones on my back, the warmth of the late afternoon sun and the shelter of the valley seemed good after the blustering hilltops. I said hello again to a little girl lying on top of the stone wall round an isolated cottage as I passed by to my car. She had been lying there when I set out four hours before, watching the empty road. She seemed to accentuate how forsaken Prescelly is now.

I felt that my exploration of Mount Prescelly had set the scene for my search for the people of Stonehenge. The background of my thoughts throughout the day had been of religion and magic at Stonehenge and Avebury, and what form it took; of far-voyaging in the European Bronze Age for the new metals, possession of which gave power, as we know from the *Iliad*. Above all, I had been thinking of Britain as a barbarian corner of a literate Europe that had Agamemnon, Jason, Zeus and Hera, whose familiar personalities and deeds have come down to us through more than three thousand years.

REFERENCES

1. Homer (Trans. E. V. Rieu), *The Iliad*, Penguin, 1950.
2. Apollonius of Rhodes (Trans. E. V. Rieu), *The Voyage of Argo*, Penguin, 1959.

CHAPTER 2

Stonehenge and Mycenae

'. . . Stonehenge . . . is unique. . . . Such a unique object postulates a unique event, and I feel sure that we must look to the literate civilisations of the Mediterranean for the inspiration and indeed for the actual execution under the hands and eyes of some trader or mission from that region.' Dr J. F. S. Stone[1]

A MAN is faced with a problem. He is a civilised man with a logical mathematical mind. In the past he has absorbed some of the techniques of Daedalus and carried through minor architectural works. He is familiar with the summits that architecture can achieve – the Palace of Minos, the great walls of Tiryns and many other magnificent buildings of his own world in the eastern Mediterranean.

He now finds himself, an adventurer in search of metal and amber with a stock of gaudy beads, wine and other goods to trade, at the court of the most powerful king in northern Europe. Everything has prospered for this king and his ancestors for several generations. The lush pastures of the plain around the king's capital have begun to bear the many herds of cattle that their potential warranted. These herds are the basis of the wealth of the king and his aristocracy, but their wealth is made superabundant by the success of their hard-headed trading in gold, bronze, amber and valuable stone. It is an age of hope and rapid change, and men look for new gods to account for it. The warrior élite swagger with their new weapons and that of their caste, the stone battle-axe, and need a god of war to swagger at their head. The goddess who comes up from the Underworld with green corn each spring does not match their arrogant desires, even if she still satisfies those of the common people, remote tribesmen and slaves. This earthbound goddess arouses contempt in the aristocracy, whose people since time immemorial have looked up to the sky for their gods as they have spread across from the plains of south-east Europe.

The king now sees himself as the high priest of a god; in fact, incited by the awed regard of his subjects, as the god himself. To express this new age and his royal omnipotence, the adventurer from the Mediterranean, who has described wonderful buildings of shaped masonry in the world from which he has come, shall execute such a building for him, the king, the god, whose displeasure means death. No other god-king in northern Europe would have such a temple. It would be a unique display of his power.

Faced with very great difficulties, the adventurer-architect seeks for inspiration for a design that would be practicable in this situation. He can only expect semi-skilled assistance from some of his crew who are civilised like himself. The large labour force he has been promised by the king will be barbarians, incapable, until some of the more intelligent are trained, of the skilled mason's work required. The most suitable building material is sarsen stone – a stone harder than granite – lying in its natural state in enormous slabs on the downs twenty miles to the north of the site commanded by the king. This site is already the most holy temple in Britain, sanctified by the presence of the Bluestones, and set in the king's capital, with his royal buildings, his ceremonial avenues and the tombs of his predecessors.

The architect's mind moves further and further along a path of compromise between the architecture he is used to and the confines of the barbarian environment he has to work in. At last, he thinks of the gates of Mycenae. This is the inspiration he is looking for. There shall be two great shaped stone pillars with a stone lintel across their tops. He will use this architectural form as a repeated motif for the temple of this barbarian king.

He draws up a plan, using his secret calculations; and then, the plan giving some hint of the power of his design, longs to see it expressed in stone. He knows that no man had previously designed such a building, and with its strange forceful design and the labour it would require to execute, no man will ever dare to repeat it.

Such labour was never known before and has not been known since. Driven by the king, the architect and the fervour of the new ascendant god, men strain to move the stones, the largest of which needs an army of one thousand five hundred before it groans forward on its sledge and rollers on its twenty-four-mile journey. Many are maimed and killed by the unstable, monstrous, moving stones. But this labour is as nothing compared to the shaping of the adamant stones which yield only a little dust at each crashing blow of the sarsen mauls. Metal tools are useless. Unyielding bronze is forced to yield to this malignant stone. The shaping is the greatest labour.

Year follows year. At last a day comes when the architect suddenly sees his creation as a whole, near completed. It stands in mute, still stone; but he sees lurking in it a king's lust for power, and his own driving ambition, and the death and labour built into the stones.

The holy inaugural feast of consecration takes place, and the architect carves the shape of the Mycenaean dagger at his belt on the pillar by the king's place, so that his mark will be on his creation for evermore.

The king epitomises the wealth of his land on this day. He wears a plate of gold on his breast, and a cape of gold on his shoulders. On his head is a helmet of bronze with nodding plumes. At his throat are amber beads and the priceless blue beads that the architect-trader brought with him. He orders axes, the divine symbol of himself and the god, to be carved beside the architect's dagger, and allows the symbol of the Mother of the Earth to be carved on a lowlier stone.

The sacrifice is made to the warrior god of the sky, and libations poured from the sacred amber cups.

The sun sinks over the western rim of the plain on a day when the prehistoric people of Britain reached their zenith of power and wealth.

Is this story fanciful? Certainly, in part, as no written document has come down to us to give detail of such a trader from the Mediterranean or such a king. But all the rapidly accumulating recent evidence added to the old, points to this *sort* of picture being the true one.

The great wealth and trading success of the Stonehenge society is proved above all by Stonehenge itself. A barbaric community which can provision a minimum of one thousand five hundred men (required for the one task of hauling stone 56, which weighs around fifty tons), who are not producing food themselves, for a considerable period, is a community living far above subsistence level.

Aside from this, grouped on the downs around Stonehenge are the tombs of its builders – archaeologically the finest barrow collections in Britain. The finery of the builders of Stonehenge in life is attested by the richness of their grave-goods, which were never expected to be recovered. The man buried, for instance, in Bush Barrow, which stands eleven feet high on Normanton Down, half a mile south of Stonehenge, had a skilfully worked lozenge-shaped plate of gold, measuring $7\frac{1}{4}$ by $6\frac{1}{4}$ inches, attached to the clothing of his breast, and a belt furnished with a large hook of gold secured to a heavy gold plate. This great personage had three bronze daggers interred with him, the handle of one of which was designed in chevrons with thousands of gold pins, and another smaller lozenge-shaped gold plate found probably ornamented a wood and leather dagger sheath, traces of which remained. A bronze axe was wrapped in cloth, and bronze rivets above the head suggest a helmet. Who can doubt that this was a royal burial? His sceptre, mounting a rare type of fossiliferous limestone from Devon, with wood and ornamental bone shaft, was laid with him.

In assessing the value at that time of the bronze objects, it should be borne in mind that, although bronze has never exceeded regal gold in esteem, its prestige in the Bronze Age was enormous. Apart from any other consideration, the far-distant trading involved in the bringing together of copper and tin, which is of isolated occurrence, guaranteed this. In the *Iliad*, the gifts passing between the royal heroes of the wealthiest peoples in Europe, and intended to be as munificent as possible, are frequently of bronze.

In the Normanton Down collection alone, one of the many within a two-mile radius of Stonehenge, other excavated barrows covered more bronze daggers, blue beads from the lands of the Eastern Mediterranean (the 'gaudy beads' of the trader-architect), amber beads, amber discs mounted in gold, and other trinkets and buttons in amber and gold. The value of the blue beads, made by a complex process by a distant civilised people, to barbarians needs no stressing (the gold and ivory traded from Africa for cheap beads in the last century is a parallel). Neither does the trading potential of the barbarians in attracting a marked concentration of the beads to themselves from such a distance, almost inconceivably, in the second millennium before Christ. All the other grave offerings I have mentioned from Normanton Down, except those of wood, leather and cloth material, come also from regions and lands far removed from Wessex.

Burials from other parts in this period, known as the period of the Wessex Culture of the Early Bronze Age by archaeologists, because it has its focus in Wessex, contained amber and gold cups, a sceptre studded with gold, a scarcely credible gold shoulder-cape, bronze helmets and dress-pins, and a wealth of variety in gold ornaments and buttons. These items are all of materials highly coveted by the wealthiest societies of Bronze Age Europe, as the contents of the Shaft Graves of the kings of Mycenae testify.

The evidence that Stonehenge was designed and its building directed by a man from Greece is again based firstly on Stonehenge itself. Stonehenge, as we see it now, is the ruin of a building of true architectural design. Nowhere else in Europe at this time was there a tradition of architectural construction, except in the Mycenaean and Cretan civilisations. These, the earliest in Europe, had arisen fundamentally as the first stage of a radiation of cultural skills from Egypt and the Middle Eastern civilisations. Nowhere else in Europe north of the Alps is there an architectural building at this period comparable with Stonehenge. It seems unlikely that skill in architecture could have made this jump from south-east to north-west Europe unaided.

The plan of the building – a highly intricate calculation – was based on four symmetrical stations, all marked at one time by stones inside the encircling bank. The ring of stone uprights was placed symmetrically with their centres at intervals of 10½ feet. They exhibit 'entasis', a curving taper, aimed to achieve an appearance of straightness. The lintel stones resting on the uprights are tongue-and-grooved to one another, and also jointed to the uprights by mortise-and-tenons, a similar technique to that adopted at the Postern Gate at Mycenae. A striking architectural refinement is that these lintels are not straight. Each has been shaped to take its individual part in the curve of the circle.

The most refined architectural feature is that the lintel stones of the inner horseshoe setting are wider at their tops than their bases to correct the apparent distortion produced by perspective.

These techniques are truly architectural and reason must assert that they would have been beyond the knowledge and skill of barbarians living on the side of Europe far from the only civilised centres. The inference is, therefore, that a man from one of these civilised countries was responsible for the construction of Stonehenge.

The possibility of this fascinating, perhaps one might even say thrilling, link with Greece was dramatically strengthened by Professor R. J. C. Atkinson's astonishing discovery in 1953 of the dagger carving on stone 53 of Stonehenge (the 'architect's mark'). This was one of the most exciting moments in archaeology, which I will describe more fully later. The dagger portrayed is not shaped like those of British type, but is similar to daggers found in the fabulously rich Shaft Graves of Mycenae, dating from 1600–1500 BC; and this similarity occurs in spite of the fact that the Mycenaean narrow, angular form was harder to produce in the sarsen medium. There were, also, adjacent carvings of bronze axes, which are of the unmistakable contemporary type traded in north-west Europe in the Early Bronze Age.

The carvings as a whole, actually on the monument itself, produced strong proof of the main period of use of this extraordinary structure – with other evidence, concluding the speculations of centuries.

Once again the finger points from Stonehenge to the civilisations of the Mediterranean; this time more specifically to Mycenae, 'rich in gold' – as Homer described it.

The other major point of evidence that, at least, a Mycenaean was in Britain and therefore could have built Stonehenge is perhaps the most satisfying in that it brings the well-known personality of a named man into a sort of indirect relationship with Stonehenge. Jason's quest for the Golden Fleece is often regarded quite sensibly as an allegory based on the intensive distant voyaging from Greece around the mid-second millennium BC in avid search of metals, particularly gold. *The Voyage of Argo* is written in the language of poetry, and it is quite impossible to trace throughout just where Jason and his crew did go. But it is clear that they voyaged to the Black Sea, their objective, and into Africa; and northward into Europe on the great rivers, where they reached the sunless land of amber; and along the southern European coast to Elba. Did a man like Jason seek the 'Golden Fleece' from the wealthy traders of Irish gold on Salisbury Plain? The archaeological evidence says that he probably did.

Scattered along just these routes are trails of faience beads. Faience is a composite material, allied to glass, and manufactured by a complex process. At the time of Stonehenge it was being produced at high pressure both for home use and trade particularly in Egypt, as the factory sites demonstrate, and also on a large scale in

Greece. These faience beads are those I have previously referred to as the blue beads from the Eastern Mediterranean in the Normanton Down barrows near Stonehenge, and as the gaudy beads of the architect-trader.

The trails of faience beads lead from the Eastern Mediterranean up the Volga and Ural Rivers to Siberia, along the Nile deep into Africa and up the Danube to Poland. Pleasingly to anyone wishing to visualise a recognisable man in the past at Stonehenge – and I, personally, am amongst that number – another trail of beads leads along southern France and the Atlantic coasts of Spain and France up to Brittany. Land's End, with its tin, has its quota as would be expected, and there is a scatter of the beads on the coasts of Britain and Ireland. A distribution map of the faience beads in Britain then shows a trail leading up from the Dorset coast to the greatest concentration, the dots overlapping they are so close together, around Stonehenge.

Was Britain another Colchis, land of the Golden Fleece? It is only fair to say that I have met archaeologists – a very small number – who are sceptical. And who shall blame them? They point to such things as the hazards of early navigation, and the sketchy engravings on the Cretan seals, which could indicate craft which were not highly seaworthy (the actual vessels might have been very different, as we shall see). No doubt, some in the future will look back and disbelieve that early astronauts could travel in such crazy spacecraft. What could actuate such men? The basic, subtle spurs to mankind have never changed. One spur is glory, and the fame of the Argonauts has lived for three and a half thousand years.

In some matters I can never be an admirably austere archaeologist, and I feel that this is one of those theories which would be historically exciting if it were true. To put it quite plainly, I would like it to be true (a dangerous attitude in archaeology). It would be a revelation, like the cleaning of a fine, esteemed old picture that begins to reveal to the cleaner the totally unexpected colour, genius, and magnificence of a Rembrandt. The Bronze Age prehistory of Britain would no longer be that of voiceless bones and stones. Faintly the voice of Homer could be heard, and Jason would say, 'Argo has been fitted out as a ship should be. All is in order and ready for the voyage.'[2]

It is a source of pleasure to me that I can follow Professors Atkinson and Stuart Piggott and Dr Stone in this. They collaborated in five seasons' excavations of Stonehenge on behalf of the unromantic Ministry of Works. At the end, they concluded that Stonehenge was designed and built by an architect from Greece, and they have carried informed opinion with them.

Surely there is no more stimulating thought in Britain's prehistory. Heracles sails once more on his Tenth Labour to distant islands in Ocean Stream, and a man like Odysseus shields his eyes from the salt sea spray, not of the tideless Inland Sea, but of the treacherous Atlantic.

We must not be carried away by the lures of the myths and desert the cold facts of archaeology, but the meeting of the two forms a picture of people as they were when they lived, breathed and laughed. Greek archaeology is given life and warmth by its myths. The truth of gods' names and men's basic attitudes comes out of them, if nothing else – and of course there is much else. The recent decipherment of the Mycenaean Linear B tablets by the late Michael Ventris, if it has done something to modify our views of Homer's pantheon of gods, has done far more to confirm them. These Greek deities of the second millennium BC truly existed, and they conditioned the thoughts and actions of a man who was there when Stonehenge was built.

REFERENCES

1. Stone, J. F. S., *Wessex before the Celts*, Thames and Hudson, 1958.
2. Apollonius of Rhodes (Trans. E. V. Rieu), *The Voyage of Argo*, Penguin, 1959.

CHAPTER 3

Indo-European Myth

'... *there was no room for fear in Achilles' heart and he sprang at the Trojans with his terrible war-cry.*' THE ILIAD[1]

JASON'S QUEST for the Golden Fleece is a particular and famous myth. Myths in general are archetypal tales which once formed the religious and historic consciousness of people, exactly as, for instance, the story of Moses is significant to us.

Like a cathedral, Stonehenge was a centre where solemn ritual perpetuated the beliefs and traditions of its people. But mythology has nothing to tell us directly of Stonehenge. All record has been lost.

This is tantalising as the monument's outstanding nature indicates with little doubt the greatest centre of power in north-west Europe. Therefore it becomes an enthralling search to delve really deep into mythology to find what does seem relevant to Stonehenge.

Three of the great mythologies are Greek, Indian and Celtic. Widely separated as these peoples were, their myths have astonishing kinship, and one might suspect that some of the lost myths of Stonehenge were similarly related, if for no other reason than that the monument lies in the same large geographic area.

A selected myth from each of these three mythologies, Greek, Indian and Celtic, will not only illustrate their affinity, but will also show a very individual approach to the supernatural that is one basis of them all. The common attitude revealed to magic (which was the objective of ancient religion) could have been shared at Stonehenge.

To take the Greek myth first: King Agamemnon, after his return from the Trojan War, was slain by his wife. The particularly strange circumstances of his death were that he was killed as he stepped from the bath; that a net was thrown over him, and that the event occurred in the bath-house annexe of the palace. His state therefore was one of being neither wet nor dry, neither clothed nor unclothed, and neither in the palace nor out of it. It is the reiteration of 'neither . . . nor' that is significant. Here we have an unusual set of 'in-betweens', as it were, in Greece – 'neither wet nor dry' and so on. The situation appears contrived; more allied to ritual than to hot-blooded murder.

If we leave Greece and turn to an Indian myth, we find that the foremost god, Indra, was defeated by a demon, who released him on condition that he agreed in the future not to slay him by day or by night, with a staff or a bow, with the flat of the hand or fists, or with anything wet nor dry. Indra later kills the demon on a sea-shore at evening by hurling sea-foam at him in which was the spirit of the god Vishnu.

Again, the 'betwixt-and-betweens' are supplied by the evening being neither night nor day, and by foam being neither wet nor dry. For good measure, the slaying takes place on the shore; that is, neither sea nor land, but where they meet.

The famous slaying of the king, Lleu Llaw, in the Welsh myth took place neither in a house nor outside, neither on horseback nor on foot, neither in water nor on land, neither clothed nor unclothed. He is killed on the river-bank under a thatched frame with one foot in a bath and one on a he-goat, half-dressed as he steps out. Again, the 'in-between' conditions are fulfilled. As in the Indian myth, the location of the slaying is where land and water meet, but this time on the river-bank. The death of the two kings, Agamemnon and Lleu Llaw, is engineered by their wives. This is a recurrent theme, with the consort or female companion of some kind playing a prominent part in the circumstances of the death of the king or hero. We will see later that by this role in the myth the female consort is to be equated with the nature goddess.

The common factor (an extremely distinctive one) in these three myths is that the situation of the magical happenings recounted is delicately insinuated between alternatives. The state is one of 'in-betweenness' that opens the door to strange events in each case. A chink has been found in the armour of the everyday world leading through to the supernatural. That the supernatural significance of the state of 'in-betweenness' was general to the beliefs of Greece,

India and the lands of the Celts is shown again by the frequency of myths centring on swans. These are creatures of neither the land, nor the water, nor the air – but of all three.

This conception of 'betweenness' cleaving into the supernatural world is particularly strong in Irish mythology. The greatest festival of their calendar, Samaine, the New Year's eve, lay in Irish belief in a limbo between the two years – a time which was a part of neither, a chink in the armour. The kings of Ireland sat around the High King of Tara in his palace on this night to repel the armies of demons who marched out from the Otherworld of the fairy mounds. In this case it is the supernatural forces that break their way through the chink into the everyday world, and not the reverse.

Extraordinary awe is engendered by the portentous births of gods and heroes often being the result of incest. The offspring, destined for great events, is thus singled out as being both son and brother to his mother, or some other anomaly according to the incestuous relationship. This is another variation of the 'neither . . . nor' state.

The sacred regard of the druids for mistletoe, attested historically by classical writers, arises from the same conception, as this plant is an anomaly, not rooted in soil, but growing on a tree between sky and earth. In myth, the Scandinavian and Germanic god, Balder, is slain by a dart of mistletoe. The strength of these beliefs is revealed by the fact that many charms even now, such as the washing of the face in dew, which is neither sea nor river, nor rain water and therefore magical, have a direct descent from them.

The scholars, Alwyn and Brinley Rees, write about this whole conception in their recent book, *Celtic Heritage*, 'It is along this knife-edge line between being and non-being that the gods appear, and the impossible becomes possible'.[2] One does not have to agree with all they have written, to feel the truth of this statement.

This way of regarding and invoking the supernatural is too subtle for archaeology ever to prove (failing some unpredictable new discovery), but I have little doubt that it activated men's minds at Stonehenge. We are on speculative ground here, but get on firm ground again when we compare the gods of the Indian *Rig Veda*, the battle hymns of conquest dating back from the region of 1300 BC, with those of the Greek myths of about the same period, and earlier.

The lord of the Olympian gods of Greece was Zeus. The meaning of the word 'Zeus' is 'bright sky'. The cognate Indian word for 'bright sky' is 'Dyaus', and he also was a god. But it is the obvious resemblance between the two words themselves, 'Zeus' and 'Dyaus', that illustrates the link between the two languages. An even closer link emerges from the comparison of the powers of the gods. In Indian mythology, Indra, the warrior god *par excellence*, is the foremost deity. The weapon he wielded was the thunderbolt – the lightning flash. This, of course, was also the dreaded weapon which gave Zeus his omnipotence over his turbulent fellow Olympians and man. So a strong cross-link existed in the specific powers of the gods.

It must be apparent that there was some deep-set connexion underlying the traditions of Greece and India, for we now have in the two mythologies, firstly, similar ways of invoking the supernatural; secondly, the most powerful gods in both cases being gods of the sky and more particularly wielding the thunderbolt; and thirdly, a relationship in the actual language used to name the gods.

The factor of language provides the clue. It has long been known that nearly all the languages of Europe and those of Persia and India are closely related. For a century or more scholars have grouped these languages into the term Indo-European. The evidence suggests that the originators of the widespread speech of these languages spread out from the steppes north of the Black Sea and of the Caucasus Mountains. These originators of languages are known loosely as Indo-Europeans, and an archaeological picture is forming of them as herdsmen, the first tamers of the horse, with their military power based in the chariot, and of their traditional and symbolic weapon, the battle-axe.

The spread of these chariot peoples is comparatively easy to follow into the land of the Hittites and Persia, and on into India where the archaeological findings in the overrun cities of the Indus valley correlate well with the hymns of conquest, the *Rig Veda*. The struggles of the warrior-god Indra with dark demons extol the victorious invasion of the Indo-Europeans, who called themselves Aryans in this sphere. The date of this invasion was in the region of 1300 BC. The entry of Greek-speaking Indo-Europeans into Greece can be placed tentatively around 2000 BC. At what date did Indo-Europeans arrive in Britain?

This is a question highly important to this book and I can call on no greater authority than Professor R. J. C. Atkinson to state his view. He writes:

> 'These invaders (into Britain from across the North Sea, *Author*) seem to be offshoots from yet another great group of Continental cultures, extending across the great plain of northern Europe from the steppes of Russia to the Rhine, and characterised as the Corded-Ware-Battle-axe cultures from their common use of impressed cord ornament on pottery and of perforated stone battle-axes as weapons. It is these peoples, among whom an element of martial display and warlike panoply suggests the institution of chieftainship, that are commonly supposed to have introduced to the West the Indo-European speech which lies at the foundation of most European languages today.'[3]

The date of the entry of these battle-axe users into Britain is still tentative but cannot be far removed from 1700 BC.

It would clearly be wrong to picture a nomadic horde setting off from the Russian steppes and travelling the vast distance across Europe unchanged into Britain. But it does seem probable that people, in particular battle-axe-using warriors, were invading Britain, and they had ancestral traditions common to the Indo-Europeans in their minds. And these battle-axe users seem to have played a powerful role in the fusion of cultures which led to the extraordinary upsurge at the time of the final building of Stonehenge.

So now we have a theatre in which to mount at least a shadow show of the human life of Stonehenge. Even the magnificence of Stonehenge could seem dwarfed and provincial on the fringe of this fascinating and colourful Indo-European backcloth, with the ancient Greeks and Persians near the centre of the picture, not to mention the Hittites (whose ruling class was Indo-European), and the dashing, chariot-mounted figure of Indra drawing the eye to the eastern end. And yet the grandiose architecture of Stonehenge can still attract the eye. It is only the human story – the myths of Stonehenge – that is so sadly lacking.

What are some of the inborn traditions of the Indo-Europeans that would be expected to illustrate life at Stonehenge? Perhaps the strongest is that of the warrior. With their chariots, the Indo-Europeans were militarily dominant wherever they went. The god, Indra, exemplifies the warrior in India, and of course there can be no more illustrious Greek warrior than the peerless Achilles of Homer's *Iliad*. In Ireland, the heroic champion of Ulster, Cu Chulainn, is out of the very same mould.

The warrior tradition has social implications as well as those of war, the warrior being an aristocrat close to his king and taking his place high in a heroic society graded from royalty and priests to free farmers, bards, bondsmen, slaves and the like. This rigid stratification of society has persisted in India from the days of the myths in the system of caste, and something of its structure can also be seen in ancient literature in Homer's royal court of Odysseus at Ithaca. The Indo-European warrior in myth is no mere rough-spun killer. In his youth he was trained in the aristocratic arts and graces of the day – poetry, music, the standards to observe for hospitable entertainment, to mention but some.

There are no documents describing the warrior tradition of Stonehenge, but it could not be more fully proved than in the archaeological record of Britain with the warrior buried under his great round barrow in aristocratic solitude, the head of his battle-axe before his eyes, and his arrogant finery still adorning his person in death. These solitary warrior burials in Britain contrast sharply with the multiple burials in long barrows of the preceding period. Homer's description of the funeral rites and barrow-burial of the hero, Patroclus, friend of Achilles, during the Trojan War, brings life to the factual findings of excavations of barrows in Britain.

Homer speaks across the millennia:

> 'In the middle of the procession Patroclus was carried by his own men . . . Behind them Prince Achilles supported the head, as the chief mourner, who was despatching his highborn comrade to the Halls of Hades'.

Homer goes on later:

> '. . . and all night long the swift Achilles, using a two-handled cup which he replenished from a golden mixing-bowl, poured out libations, drenched the earth with wine, and called on the spirit of the unhappy Patroclus'.

Then Achilles himself says to the other heroes according to Homer:

> 'As for his barrow, I do not ask you to construct a very large one, something that is seemly but no more. Later you can build a big and high one . . .'.[4]

Homer, writing it is thought around 800 BC, recreates the funeral of a Bronze Age Mycenaean hero, who was of ancestral Indo-European origin, somewhere in the region of 1260 BC – the probable time of the Trojan War.

Turning from the warrior to another aspect: Indo-European society was quite unlike the contemporary societies of early crop-growing communities. The latter agriculturists grouped themselves in largely undifferentiated peasant tribes, whereas the Indo-Europeans, with their pastoral herds mainly of cattle, were ruled by powerful kings. Above all others, Agamemnon, King of Men (as Homer describes him), demonstrates this power throughout the *Iliad*, and the confirmation has been found in the extraordinary wealth – bespeaking power – of the royal burials at Mycenae. Mycenaean society was focused on cities, of course, but the richly furnished graves of pastoral chieftains north of the Caucasus Mountains probably reveal ancestrally this tradition of powerful kingship.

The way tribal prosperity is bound to the well-being of the king is shown in the myths of Indo-European countries, as is the beneficial fertility resulting from his ritual slaying. Some of the 'royal' barrows in Britain, such as Bush Barrow (see p. 12), very conceivably commemorate such dramatic events at Stonehenge, Avebury and other ritualistic centres of religion and kingship.

Not only worldly power was vested in the king, but the magical element of personifying the prosperity of his people. The myths such as those quoted above of Lleu Llaw in Wales and Agamemnon in Greece are accepted by most authorities as descriptions of actual ritual in the performance of which the king placed himself in a situation where he was magically vulnerable. If he was ageing or his powers were waning in any way, he was slain and succeeded by another. Many myths, in which an old hag seeks an embrace from a bold young warrior and on this being granted becomes transformed into a beautiful maiden, illustrate the succession of the new king. The hag-maiden is the territorial nature goddess whom the new king must wed. At one time in Irish mythological history her actual name was Sovereignty. One visualises a ceremony in which a magically potent woman sheds a disguise and there follows symbolic, or possibly actual, coupling between her and the king.

In Ireland, the young warrior Niall of the Nine Hostages embraces an old hag who immediately changes to the most beautiful woman in the world. He asks who she is; she replies, 'King of Tara, I am Sovereignty . . . and your seed shall be over every clan'.[5]

Scholars have demonstrated that the offering of a magically potent drink by the goddess to the king was a part of Indo-European ritual. The great mythical Queen Medb of Connaught, whose name is related to 'mead' and 'drink', offered drink to many kings at their inauguration in Ireland. In Indian myth, Indra drank Soma (the drink of the gods) from the mouth of his consort.

The ritual slaying of the ageing or blemished king is a sacrifice, and sacrifice played an all-important part in the day-to-day life of the Indo-Europeans as well as at their festivals. The sacrifice was normally an animal, though human sacrifice was not unknown. Seers and sages played important roles in these rituals. Quantities of cattle bones have been excavated in the area of Woodhenge, which is two miles north-east of Stonehenge, and I believe that many a fine bull met its sacrificial end here.

But, above all, the world of the Indo-European was a man's world – the world of the aristocratic warrior. The two great exemplars of this in myth are Achilles of Greece and Cu Chulainn of Ireland. Regarding Cu Chulainn, Kenneth Hurlstone Jackson, who is Professor of Celtic at Edinburgh University, has written in his recent book, *The Oldest Irish Tradition*, 'The coincidence with Achilles is striking'.[6] He points out that both the tales of the Irish champion and the Greek hero in the *Iliad* deal almost exclusively with the warrior class, the remainder being treated as a rabble. The ideas and ideals in both cases are those of aristocratic warriors. Next that both heroes are greedy for fame above all else. Cu Chulainn says this when confronted with a specific choice between a short life on the one hand and fame on the other:

> 'Provided that I shall be famous I do not care if I last in this world for only a single day.'[7]

This statement epitomises Cu Chulainn, whose devastating power in battle is dedicated in all its overwhelming force to Ulster.
The resemblance is obvious to Achilles, who says:

> 'My divine Mother, Thetis of the Silver Feet, says that Destiny has left two courses open to me on my journey to the grave. If I stay here and play my part in the siege of Troy, there is no homecoming for me, though I shall win undying fame.'[8]

Achilles chooses to stay and die.

One might say that these parallels are rather general, and merely show ideals common to all warrior heroes. But then Professor Kenneth Hurlstone Jackson demonstrates a really extraordinary coincidence between comparatively minor incidents in the stories of the two heroes.

Ulster and Connaught are at war, and Professor Jackson writes:

> '. . . there is a striking scene in the Cattle Raid of Cooley (the myth dealing with the war, *P.C.*) where Cu Chulainn comes upon a Connaught charioteer who is cutting wood to replace a broken chariot-pole. The man does not know him, and, taking him for one of his own people, asks his help in stripping the bark and twigs from the poles he has cut. Presently he discovers who his fellow-worker is, and gives himself up for lost, but Cu Chulainn tells him not to be afraid, for he never kills charioteers. Here the coincidence is remarkable with the scene in the *Iliad* where Achilles catches one of the sons of Priam cutting wood for a chariot rail . . .'[9]

'One of the sons of Priam' is a Trojan with whom the Greek Achilles is at war.

I think it is significant that the chariot relationship figures so largely in these two corresponding myths, and to my mind they could stem from an archetypal story common to the Indo-European heritage in which the chariot played such a preponderant part. So too, I would add to Professor Jackson's correlations of the two heroes, the weeping of Achilles' immortal chariot-horses at the death of his friend Patroclus, against the weeping of Cu Chulainn's chariot-horse, the Grey of Macha, as an omen of his death. Mytho-archaeological evidence reveals a specific common method in the construction of chariot wheels in India, Greece and Celtic Britain with single-piece bent felloes.

On this theme, Alwyn and Brinley Rees write:

> 'Each of these four cycles (groups of the Irish myths, *P.C.*) contains material which appears to belong to a common Indo-European heritage and which presumably was part of the tradition of the Celtic peoples before they ever came to these islands (the British Isles, *P.C.*)'.[10]

It seems possible that it was tales such as these, archetypal in forming the Achilles and Cu Chulainn myths themselves – the myth behind the myth – that Battle-axe warriors carried into Britain from Europe at the time of Stonehenge.

I find something haunting in this comparison of Cu Chulainn and Achilles – the one of our own native islands and the other on the windy plain of Troy by the Dardanelles. The meeting of Cu Chulainn and Achilles seems to transcend time and place and span the world with a fierce warrior sadness. No less haunting can be the thought of the pathetic, inert warrior bones under many barrows in Britain compared with the time when they were clothed with powerful flesh and spurred by unconquerable spirit, such as Cu Chulainn's and Achilles', when they might have said:

> 'Am I not big and beautiful, the son of a great man, with a goddess for my Mother? Yet Death and Soveran Destiny are waiting for me too. A morning is coming, or maybe an evening or a noon, when somebody is going to kill me too in battle with a cast of his spear or an arrow from his bow.'[11]

Here is the boasting of a hero, mystically endued with power from a strange birth, fatalistically enduring and courageous, of immense physical power – an aristocratic Indo-European warrior, whose shade may be sensed at Stonehenge. With him and his fellow nobles in the majestic building is the High-king attended by the wise men, and through the magic person of the High-king the narrow, ritualistic cleft was found into the supernatural where the great gods of the sky could be propitiated and the desires of he and his people realised by the power of magic. Quietly the priestess watched in this world of men. The festival at which it had been decided that the King must die would come, and then the fertile power of woman would give potency to a new king.

REFERENCES

1. Homer (Trans. E. V. Rieu), *The Iliad*, Penguin, 1950.

2. Rees, Alwyn and Rees, Brinley, *Celtic Heritage*, Thames and Hudson, 1961.

3. Atkinson, R. J. C., *Stonehenge*, Hamish Hamilton, 1956.

4. Homer (Trans. E. V. Rieu), *op. cit.*

5. Rees, Alwyn and Rees, Brinley, *op. cit.*

6. Jackson, Kenneth Hurlstone, *The Oldest Irish Tradition: A Window on the Iron Age*, Cambridge University Press, 1964.

7. Rees, Alwyn and Rees, Brinley, *op. cit.*

8. Homer (Trans. E. V. Rieu), *op. cit.*

9. Jackson, Kenneth Hurlstone, *op. cit.*

10. Rees, Alwyn and Rees, Brinley, *op. cit.*

11. Homer (Trans. E. V. Rieu), *op. cit.*

CHAPTER 4

Sky God and Great Goddess

I COULD see the dagger-carving from fifty yards away as I walked towards Stonehenge on a grey October morning. Then I could see the axe-carvings as I approached nearer.

If my presence were transposed in time and place, my approach could be compared with an approach to the High Altar with its Cross in Westminster Abbey. I pictured myself standing in Westminster Abbey with a consciousness in my mind of all the other great public buildings, processional ways, and houses for its population that would then lie around me in London – Buckingham Palace, the Mall, the City. But on Stonehenge and its buildings a wind has been blowing for every second of every day for three and four thousand years – just as it gusted on my face – blowing them away as dust, smoothing down the mounds of banks and barrows, except for the defiant, harder-than-granite columns of Stonehenge itself, which stands as a climax of interest to archaeologists studying barbarian Britain, and as a superb zenith of achievement and pride to those barbarians themselves who built and performed ritual in it.

I stood and thought as if I were a Stonehenge man.

Half a mile to my north, almost from horizon to horizon, runs the old Processional Way to the ancient Temple-tomb, still used by the priestesses and common people who worship the Great Goddess. I live beyond the old Temple-tomb in the town whose walls run down a combe almost to the banks of the River Avon. Many of the freemen I know live outside the town along by the Avon.

On the hill to one side of the combe of the town stands the King's Palace. From many parts of the town, its high massive timber walls show dark silhouettes against the southern sky.

Where I stand now is outside the new Temple of the God of the Sky, which I will never enter, but I know that inside the King, guided by his priests and wise men, performs ceremonies which will please the gods, so that this new age of peace and plenty will continue. We are used to watching the King and his court walk up the New Processional Way from the river to the Temple of the God of the Sky at the festivals to carry out the ceremonies.

All round the horizon, as I stand outside the new temple, I can see the dome-shaped barrows of the kings and nobles of my people who have been buried there for many generations, as our genealogists tell us. The new Temple of the God of the Sky stands where the festivals of the Great Goddess used to be held before the warriors with their battle-axes came across the sea from the east with their new god whom we could see was more to be feared.

In reality, as I stood in the twentieth century with American accents and foreign tongues mingling with the British voices passing by, I knew that my thoughts in the role of a Stonehenge man had been mere guesses. And yet mainly guesses as to the specific purpose of the different public buildings – the buildings were there. An eminent archaeologist of the present time, Mr Paul Ashbee, has written, '. . . Stonehenge and its Avenue, the Cursus, Woodhenge, and Durrington Walls should be considered together as a single entity.'[1] Some of these names may not be familiar to everybody, but before I discuss these sites, I would like to say that the places Mr Ashbee mentions are those I was thinking of in my role of Stonehenge man. With the dense grouping of barrows around Stonehenge, they combine to form an area about five miles square within which one can seldom be more than a few hundred yards from a known monument of Stonehenge date. This is a unique grouping of early barbarian monuments in Britain to which only Avebury is comparable, and its social implications must surely be that here was the capital of a large area of Britain. If there were kings in Stonehenge Britain – and we have seen that the evidence certainly suggests that there were – the ruins grouped round Stonehenge might be looked on fairly, I think, as the royal capital of the High King. In general terms, Tara, the royal palace famed in Irish myth as the seat of the High King could be regarded as giving a rather similar concept in later times, although it is as well to note that the ruins of Stonehenge far outstrip those of Tara, with all the latter's mythological fame.

I looked round the windy plain. Half a mile to the north a line of large barrows along a ridge marked the near side of the Cursus.

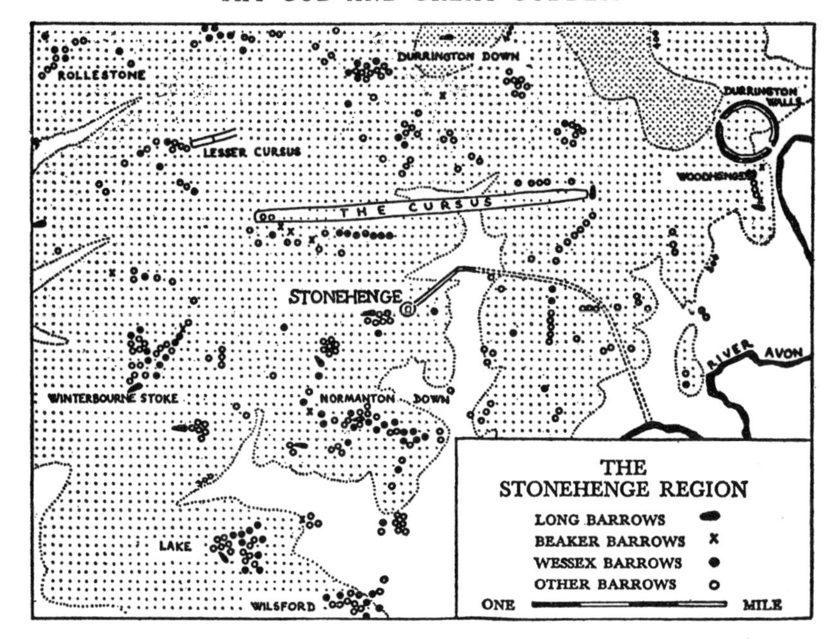

Fig. A. Map showing the concentration of ruins around Stonehenge, the greatest area of such ruins in Britain. As a group, it dates from the third to second millenia BC.

This is a ceremonial way over a mile and a half long and more than a hundred yards wide. These dimensions are greater than those of the Mall. Its sides are defined by a bank and ditch, and across its eastern end there is a long barrow dating towards the end of the Stone Age, which would have been both tomb and temple. Excavation in the ditch of the Cursus has unearthed material of the time when the first building at Stonehenge was taking place.

To the south, the impressive Normanton group of barrows with its 'royal' burial in Bush Barrow crested a ridge looking almost as if I could have thrown a cricket ball amongst them across the deceptive plain.

On the high edge of the immense chalk plateau, overlooking the River Avon, lies Woodhenge, two miles to the north-east of where I stood; and eighty yards from Woodhenge is Durrington Walls, a roughly circular enclosure of even greater area than Avebury. Archaeological finds of large quantities of bones of domesticated and wild animals and pottery show that the Woodhenge – Durrington Walls area was one of intensive human occupation that also spread down by the River Avon towards Amesbury.

What does this tract of ruins, five miles square, signify? It could be interpreted as solely a great centre of religion with Stonehenge and the other circular monuments as a group of temples. There can be no doubt that religion played an important part in the lives of the people who once used these buildings, but it may be that this importance has been over-stressed. I think it is probable that the rites and daily life of kingship were also carried out in these ruins, and this could point to at least one diversity of use of the different buildings.

The term 'henge' is a technical archaeological one deriving from 'Stonehenge', but is applied in this technical sense to the sixty or so monuments in Britain defined by a circular bank with a concentric inner ditch. This circular bank and ditch with one or more entrances constitutes a 'henge'; there need be no structure of stone as at Stonehenge. Durrington Walls and Woodhenge for instance are henges.

Mr Paul Ashbee has this to say, 'Henges and related structures have long been claimed as temples, but it is a strange society that constructs imposing groups of temples and no houses.'[2] That is the difficulty – if *all* these monuments of the Stonehenge people are temples, where did they live?

With the existing evidence, I believe that when I stood by Stonehenge I was surrounded by the ruins of a city. The use of the word 'city' referred to Stonehenge Britain may be startling, and perhaps not justifiable on all counts, but to an outlying tribesman coming to it from his village, or even say from one of the lesser centres of power in Dorset, how else would he regard it with its impressive architectural buildings and large area than as a city?

As I crossed the inner courtyard, a practical-looking man was pointing out to his wife the projecting tenon on the top of a sarsen upright, and its once fitting mortise in a lintel at his feet. 'This wasn't thrown together, you know,' he said with the spontaneous approval of a craftsman for a job well done.

I stopped in front of stone 53 and looked at the dagger- and axe-carvings in the close-textured grey stone. What did the axe-carvings symbolise? They could be mere symbols of wealth; an exulting in the possession of precious bronze. They could be a form of sympathetic magic to attract by their presence their actual metal counterparts. They could be a protection, again by sympathetic magic, for the king and his people, and the herds and crops. Perhaps they could be all these fused into the symbol of a god. In Crete at that time the two-edged double-axe was a symbol of divinity. I think the symbolism of the Stonehenge axes could be complex, just as that of the Cross. When a man of Stonehenge saw the axe symbol, a whole testament of the specific deeds and personality of an anthropomorphised god of the sky, perhaps the sun, may have crossed his mind. That the god and the sun were one would in no way tie the god to an abstract benignity of the sky. The god's exploits in the world of men could be as varied, specific and active as Apollo's in the Trojan War.

I crossed the courtyard to stone 57, which has been re-erected since Professor R. J. C. Atkinson's excavations at Stonehenge. On this stone, about seven feet from the ground, is a faint rectangular carving which has a rounded extension on its top.

Professor Atkinson writes of this carving:

> 'The religious implications of this symbol are even more important. For it seems probable that this, and other variants, are degenerate versions of a representation of a mother-goddess, whose cult is intimately associated with the Western family of neolithic cultures as a whole, but has no place in the skyward-looking eastern cultures of which the builders of Stonehenge III were the heirs in Britain. We have here one more piece of evidence for the fusion of diverse religious traditions in the final and greatest period of building at Stonehenge.'[3]

I stood in front of the ruin of the Great Trilithon, which is clearly the climactic place of Stonehenge – marked as it is by the Altar Stone, the sole stone of micaceous sandstone from Milford Haven; backed by the greatest height reached by the monument; facing the entrance; and with most attention paid to the finish of the adjacent stones. On my immediate right hand was the axe symbol, perhaps of the sky god, and on the corresponding stone to my left was the symbol of the Mother Goddess. The right hand of man has always been the dominant, and as I stood in the place of the King, so I saw the relationship of the two symbols – the new Indo-European war-god of the Sky on my dominant right, and the once all-powerful but now underlying symbol of the fertility of the Great Goddess of the Mediterranean on my left.

An imaginary line from where I stood, running forward through the entrance of Stonehenge, points with a considerable degree of accuracy to the position of sunrise on Midsummer Day. Stonehenge was a monument that was altered and adapted over a period of centuries, and this careful orientation of the axis of the monument on the Midsummer dawn was not observed in its earlier form. This may indicate new beliefs in its later builders, and once again may point to a religious revolution in Stonehenge Britain.

Many things such as the known sky-worship of Indo-Europeans, the rock-carvings of sun-symbols in Scandinavia, and the gold discs with symbolic designing found in Britain of Stonehenge date, lend support to the view that the final building of the masonry temple celebrated the relegation of the Great Goddess to a subservient position and the vaunting of the new Sky God. Accompanying this may have been a social upheaval, changing the matriarchal society of the Great Goddess, which stemmed from Crete, to a patriarchal society traditional to the Indo-Europeans, in which women played a lowly role and male gods, kings and warriors wielded power.

I walked through the colonnade and out over the smooth grass to the Aubrey Holes – now marked with circles of chalk – which run in a circle just inside the bank surrounding Stonehenge. By comparison with other henges in Britain, Professor Atkinson thinks the bank, ditch and Aubrey Holes form the earliest monument at Stonehenge, dating from very approximately 2000 BC, and that the Aubrey Holes may have been for the purpose of invoking the Great Goddess of the Earth. If this is so, one may picture the pouring of libations and the addressing of incantations into these holes. Again possible evidence of the clash of the religions of earth and sky.

My mind reacted with anger as I saw from my stance by the Aubrey Holes a large sign of the Campaign for Nuclear Disarmament on one of the colonnade stones. The daubing of this unique building which represents the paramount link with our history of three and a half thousand years ago seemed vandalism indeed. But then my mind took a more Olympian detachment, and I saw the C.N.D. sign much like a Bronze Age sun-symbol, and found something moving in this most ancient building bearing symbols that expressed the deepest fears and hopes of people so far separated in time. It seemed that destiny was being invoked from Stonehenge once again.

I walked back through the monument, which was thronged with

visitors. All round were snatches of conversation, some comprehending, but many devoid of any response to the grandeur of a building that is a tangible chapter in our history. My last visual impression of the visit was of a spotted bluestone, and I left thinking of my exploration of Mount Prescelly six months before. Was the sky god of the Indo-Europeans in Britain he who lived on Mount Prescelly? It might be so. His propitiation would bless the flow of copper axes and gold from Ireland past his holy mountain. As I had left Prescelly, I had looked back and seen Foel Trigarn silhouetted as an ominous dark cone against the Sun, who was completing his chariot ride across the sky before sinking into the Other World of the Western Sea.

REFERENCES

1. Ashbee, Paul, *The Bronze Age Round Barrow in Britain*, Phoenix House, 1960.

2. Ashbee, Paul, *op. cit.*

3. Atkinson, R. J. C., *Stonehenge*, Hamish Hamilton, 1956.

CHAPTER 5

The Second 'City'

IN THE grey light Stonehenge had seemed like a silver ship floating on an ochrous green sea. By the time I reached Woodhenge, the sun was shining brilliantly, and the wind had the smell of warmed downland grass tingeing its utter cleanness with exquisite sweetness. Patrick Leigh Fermor would have the crystalline light of Greece cut as diamonds for jewels; I would gather the wind on the downs of England and use it to scent all beautiful women; carried on it is the loveliest music, Rachmaninoff's C Minor Concerto, the Enigma Variations of Elgar. The smell of the downs is as familiar and welcome to me as that of sawdust to a carpenter. I associate it with the fascination of locating an archaeological monument deep in uninhabited downlands, and the interest and sometimes surprise there is when the site is found. On rare occasions, feeling can take wings when one discovers a new monument that sharp, trained eyes before you have missed. You have written a word – perhaps even a sentence – in history, and the sweetness of downland air re-conjures the magic.

It is possible that Squadron-Leader G. S. M. Insall, VC, had some similar sort of pleasure in 1925 when he saw from an aeroplane, two miles from Stonehenge, concentric circles of black dots. The site of these black dots became known as Woodhenge, as the dots were the post-holes for immense wooden uprights, evidence of which had survived. These were found in 1928 when the site was excavated by Mr and Mrs Cunnington. Large quantities of pottery were found contemporary with the earliest Stonehenge – the period of the bank, ditch and Aubrey Holes there – and the sacrificial burial of a child of three with a cleft skull was unearthed near the centre of the six concentric rings of post-holes. The third ring of post-holes from the outside were about six feet deep and five feet across, that is, of a size to take the trimmed whole trunks of mature forest trees.

It was at first thought that Woodhenge was an open temple of similar nature to Stonehenge, but Professor Stuart Piggott, followed by all archaeologists, now thinks it is the remains of a circular, roofed, timber building with an open, central courtyard. This building would have been large; a hundred and forty-five feet in diameter, and possibly over thirty feet in height. Its different architectural nature from Stonehenge could confirm the suggestion in the last chapter that not all 'henges' (for Woodhenge is surrounded with a bank and ditch) were necessarily used for the same purpose – that is, exclusively for religious ritual. Once a building is thought of as being roofed, one's mind begins to turn to more utilitarian uses, and the profuse debris of human life in this area leads one further along the same path. On the present evidence it would be quite wrong to say that Woodhenge was a palace; it would be equally wrong to say that it could not have been. I am sure that as archaeological knowledge increases we will know the answer. Meantime Mr Paul Ashbee has imaginatively exceeded the usual reticence of leading archaeologists, and written:

> 'With all this evidence in mind it seems likely that the builders of barrows continued to dwell amongst the barrows of their ancestors, that house and temple such as the dwellings of priest-kings at Avebury, Stonehenge, and Tara, and their subject princelings at Knowlton and other centres, were one and the same.'[1]

I drove off northwards past the banks of Durrington Walls, which run down a combe to an entrance by the Avon. This enclosure, again, so close to Woodhenge, yet so much greater in area, and in a sheltered position by the riverside, makes one think of yet another function for henges. The excavation by Dr J. F. S. Stone of '. . . a long straight line of 58 post-holes with off-sets suggestive of part of a building and associated with . . . occupational refuse . . .'[2] is evidence of habitation against its outer bank. Perhaps this is a gleam of light, because the great problem of the people of Stonehenge Britain is still where they all lived. The population must have been large by prehistoric standards, as the organised labours of building Stonehenge, Avebury and other works prove; yet we know where their ceremonies took place, and the tombs of their royal and noble dead, but there is no certain idea of the more important question historically which is – where and in what sort of building did they spend their everyday lives? No doubt, proof will come as the archaeological search goes on; perhaps even before I have finished writing this book, because the search is intense. When this happens, it will be a great day – no! – one of the greatest days in the history of British archaeology.

I drove on across the Avon at Bulford and went north up the river valley. At Milston, I turned east along a narrow downland lane and climbed for a mile or so. All human habitation ceased as is usual on the waterless downs. The tarmac suddenly ended and the way went on as a deep-rutted chalk track. At the beginning of the track was a large War Department notice warning against leaving the track and the danger of unexploded bombs lying on the ground beyond this point. I think most field archaeologists will agree that this sort of encounter is one of the charms of archaeology – certainly in retrospect. The urge to go on, to find your goal on the map, is imperative, and the hazards of warning notices such as this one add a spice to your exploration, as do firing ranges and encounters with gamekeepers, racing-stable owners, wardens and bulls; all common on remote downlands in Wessex. You do not have to cross the Gobi Desert to venture into the unknown – at least to yourself.

The deep ruts cut my speed down to a five-mile-an-hour crawl, and as I went on there was no improvement in the surface. I stopped and looked at the Ordnance map. My objective was the famous group of barrows on Silk Hill. I still had a mile to cover in the car and then half a mile on foot. The time was a quarter past three and I had an appointment with Dr Isobel Smith, the leading authority on Avebury, at Avebury at four o'clock. I had eighteen miles to cover to keep my appointment, much along twisty, river-valley lanes, so I was compelled to abandon Silk Hill.

My reason for wishing to visit the Silk Hill barrows was to continue my exploration of the barrow collections strung along the chalk ridge, ten miles long, lying between the Rivers Avon and Bourne. These collections are particularly fine and interesting and contain many special types known as bell- and disc-barrows, the tombs of the Wessex Culture chieftains who lived when the architectural structure of Stonehenge was built. But my particular interest was that this line of Wessex Culture barrows points in the direction of Avebury, as do no others. There can be not the slightest doubt that the way from Stonehenge to Avebury was being trodden constantly, and these barrows are like a finger pointing to where the head-waters of the Avon can be avoided and where the crossing of the Vale of Pewsey is easiest. I am satisfied that when a Stonehenge man journeyed to Avebury, he walked along a heavily used track on this ridge running through the communities of his compatriots.

I journeyed likewise north to Avebury, crossing the Vale of Pewsey enclosed in its great chalk bastions to north and south. And so I came to one of the most impressive and interesting groups of prehistoric ruins in northern Europe, laid out over the floor of the valley of the head-waters of the River Kennet and climbing the down slopes to the crests around, covering an area of about three miles square. I never come to these ruins without intellectual excitement – here is evidence of the earliest great social community in Britain.

There can be no doubt that the great works at Avebury were never executed by disorganised savages. Looked at in the stream of world history, here was a community with exceptional power and organisation over a wide area. Even in their dilapidation of four thousand years and more what structures these people built – the Avebury enclosure itself, which is the biggest ceremonial monument in Europe; Silbury Hill, the largest man-made mound in western Europe; the West Kennet chambered long barrow, the biggest in Britain; and many other structures scattered across the valley, still magnificent in their near utter ruin. By whom were they built?

This period of the history of people in Britain has proved to be of extraordinary complexity and it was this that attracted Dr I. F. Smith, a Canadian, to study its archaeology, particularly its pottery. In recent years, she has brought classification and chronology to the number of cultures overlapping each other at that time through meticulous study of their pottery. To the lay person, such careful analysis over a number of years of the slightest nuances of innumerable sherds of pottery from many sites may seem pedestrian; one might feel that these pieces of pottery could lead to little understanding of living people of the past. But the secrets of prehistory are hard won, and the classification of pottery according to cultures is one of the prime weapons of the archaeologist, producing order out of chaos, from which a wider and clearer picture of people and events can eventually spring.

I spent an hour and a half with Dr Smith and at the end of this time, as always in my meetings with her, my mind had advanced a little further towards her deep knowledge of the cultures of Avebury and elsewhere in Britain at that period.

The study of the time of Avebury still has far to go, and it must be remembered always that the way of thought of pre-Christian, and pre-Buddhist peoples was totally different from that of people in general now. The abstract ideal of 'Love thy neighbour' had not been uttered and did not lie in any person's mind or subconscious mind, however fallow. Friends were loved, enemies hated, and the rest of mankind fair game for whatever one's power allowed one to do to them. Morality in the sense of any regard for the fate of mankind did not exist. Darwin lay thousands of years ahead, and Avebury man had scarce any understanding of the universe and his position in it. It is not easy for the mind to break through the time barrier and return to a world ruled by the warrior and magic.

To Britain came two main streams of people, each with quite different outlooks and modes of life. The first and earlier stemmed fundamentally from the Mediterranean and the second from northern Europe; the first spread across Britain primarily from the west, and the second from the east. There was no grand military strategy, but it was as if a 'pincer movement' of peoples moved across Britain, the westward arm of the pincer coming first, and then fusion coming later as the eastward arm moved also.

So far in this book attention has been mainly on warrior people coming to Britain from the east. But the first revolutionary movement in techniques of human living had a Mediterranean origin. This, the neolithic (New Stone Age) revolution – one of the greatest advances of man – introduced agriculture, domesticated animals and pottery into Britain for the first time. Prior to this entry, at present thought to be not long before 3000 BC, man in Britain had lived only as a hunter, fisher and gatherer of food from wild sources. These immigrants throughout Britain are known as the Windmill Hill Culture, after their enclosure on Windmill Hill in the complex of structures at Avebury, which first founded the great capital.

In Dr Smith's definitive work, *Windmill Hill and Avebury* – a detailed examination of the results of centuries of study of the Avebury complex and extensive excavations, including her own – she concludes that the enormous central enclosure of Avebury was built by the descendants of the Windmill Hill people and another, later arriving, Late Neolithic people, the Rinyo-Clacton (a problematical people whom we will examine in more detail later). She thinks that people of the Beaker cultures – the north European eastward arm of the 'pincer movement', which included elements of the battle-axe users – were present while the great enclosure at Avebury was being built and played some part in the construction of the great works. Pottery has been found – some accompanying burials at the foot of standing stones in various parts of the complex – made by these three cultures, the descendants of the Windmill Hill, the Rinyo-Clacton and the Beaker. But she does not think that the Beaker people were the initiators of Avebury, in spite of the dominance they usually seem to have ultimately achieved wherever they went in Europe. There are no monuments similar to Avebury from where they came in Europe, whereas the pottery of the Windmill Hill descendants and Rinyo-Clacton culture is present in the earliest archaeological layers excavated at many monuments similar to Avebury in Britain.

Until recently Avebury was considered an expression of the determined capabilities of the Beaker cultures, talented people, who seem to have been the first to introduce worked metal into Britain, and who might be said to have first stimulated the technological revolution that continues here up to the present day. Their skill would have seemed commensurate with the colossal works at Avebury, but if, as Dr Smith thinks, one has to look elsewhere for the initiation and main execution of the stupendous undertaking – to the Windmill Hill descendants and the Rinyo-Clacton – the capabilities and power of these pre-Beaker peoples will have to be carefully investigated. As we will see later their contacts with the Mediterranean civilisations probably caused them to be no less knowledgeable and capable than the Beaker people, but the exceptional drive and determination of the Beaker people made them dominant eventually in the clash and fusion of the alien cultures.

The custom of the Beaker people of sometimes placing rich offerings with their dead – metal goods, fine pottery and so on – may have over-magnified their earlier power in Britain in the eyes of archaeologists *vis-à-vis* other Late Neolithic people who may have been equally advanced but who interred their dead without offerings.

The building of the main enclosure of Avebury alone must lead to a reassessment of the organised power of the Windmill Hill descendants and the Rinyo-Clacton. This is a colossal monument – a henge, with bank outside ditch – with a diameter from bank to bank of more than a quarter of a mile. The top of the bank – about three-quarters of a mile in circumference – was more than fifty feet in vertical height above the bottom of the ditch, the height of two average houses, one on another. There are other almost equally impressive structures as this extraordinary ditch at Avebury, as we shall see.

These people from the Mediterranean had been making their way up into Britain by land and by sea for a thousand years before the building of Avebury and the coming of the Beaker people, which in round figures started about 2000 BC. That much of the Mediterranean peoples' travelling was by sea is shown by the distribution of their monuments (mainly chambered burial tombs) up the west coast of Britain to northern Scotland, with concentrations on the islands, peninsulas and large river estuaries. In Ireland, too, their remains rival Stonehenge and Avebury in grandeur. Many centuries before the arrival of the Mycenaean faience trading beads in Britain that I described earlier in the book, there was far-distant voyaging going on up the length of the western seaboard of Europe. The emphasis of this Neolithic immigration into the British Isles is from the west. Ireland figures largely and the spread in Britain is from west to east, as the progressively later dates in this direction obtained by the scientific radio-carbon method show when applied to the earliest Neolithic sites.

So here were two great migratory streams of people of quite different religions and cultures. Was Stonehenge the symbol of their meeting, clash and fusion? Was the outcome of the meeting of the two great pincer arms expressed at Stonehenge in the axe-carvings for the Indo-European sky god, and the Mediterranean Great Goddess symbol? Was Avebury the fertility temple of the Great Goddess before the sky god came to Britain?

I said goodbye to Dr Smith and walked out into the quiet evening of the beautiful sarsen and chalk-built village, with its air of the downs, that partly spreads over prehistoric Avebury. My mind was struggling to achieve a balanced view of the archaeological evidence of more than a thousand years of our history. The rays of the sun from the west were like a deep rose limelight on the temple. The sky merged down from mother-of-pearl to peach to vivid arterial blood-red. Stubble fires flickered on Waden Hill, adding red to red. All the day's visitors had gone. Avebury was mine to explore as I wished. I walked through the outskirts of the village to the foot-bridge over the Winterbourne. From there, the truncated cone of Silbury Hill rose a mile to the south like a pudding served to Gargantua. One hundred and thirty feet high and covering five and a half acres, it is the largest mound constructed by man in western Europe. Specific archaeological evidence from it is almost entirely lacking, but it is seen as part of the ruins of the Avebury metropolis. Professor Atkinson sees it as a fitting barrow for the exceptional king who ruled when Stonehenge was built. One thing is clear; the builders of the temple circle and Silbury Hill at Avebury were a mighty people in their time. They must have been to have carried through such tasks successfully. What urged them on? No doubt, among the complex impulses, the pride of extolling their own greatness played a part, but that religion is the key may be shown by the ditch of Avebury being inside its bank. It does not seem to have been built for defence.

I walked back into the temple to the ruined ring of sarsen stones known as the South Circle. In the middle of this is a setting of stones which Dr Smith sees very tentatively as resembling the plan of a long barrow temple-tomb of the Neolithic people. If such a resemblance was intended, a large sarsen called the Obelisk, now destroyed, would be in the relative position of the burials in such a long barrow. Assuming that this stone had a phallic significance, its position at the place of death would symbolise life through death, comparable to many fertility beliefs known in comparative religion. Mr Robert Graves, the poet and mythologist, has written of one type of conception underlying the most ancient cult of fertility of life through death.

> 'The tribal Nymph, it seems, chose an annual lover from her entourage of young men, a king to be sacrificed when the year ended; making him a symbol of fertility, rather than the object of her erotic pleasure. His sprinkled blood served to fructify trees, crops and flocks. . . .'[3]

Whatever rites took place at Avebury, it seems a temple of fertility, and Mr Graves graphically expresses here a concept of life through death which may give the inspiration if not the actual detail of ritual. Parallels indicate that the nature of kingship under the Great Goddess was very different from that of the all-powerful Indo-European kings under their sky gods. These latter might be sacrificed but only after a period during which their rule was absolute. Myths arising from very ancient sources, such as that of Aphrodite and Adonis, suggest that young gods of fertility were thought of as dying at each year's end and of being born again each spring with the renewed vegetation. In this myth, Aphrodite is the Greek embodiment of the far more ancient Great Goddess, whose religion spread round the seaboards of western Europe, to have one of its most magnificent expressions in Avebury.

The West Kennet Avenue of standing stones runs from Avebury for a distance of one and a half miles to a site known as the Sanctuary on Overton Hill. Professor Piggott considers that the pattern of post-holes at the Sanctuary could be the evidence for a large timber building. What is left of the Avenue has opposed pairs of stones, one upright and straight, suggesting the male principle, and the other more lozenge-shaped and set on a corner, suggesting the female; so again the evidence points to the cult of fertility at Avebury. In Sardinia, carved standing stones occur near communal burial tombs of the Great Goddess, and there the female stones are apparent from the stylised breasts they display, as against the conical phallic shapes of the male stones of equal number.

Further evidence of the religion of the Great Goddess of the Mediterranean comes from the West Kennet Long Barrow, a mile and a quarter south of Avebury, which is another of the impressive monuments of this metropolis. It was excavated in 1955–56 by Professors Stuart Piggott and Atkinson. The gallery of this barrow is walled and roofed with very large slabs of sarsen stone, and runs forty feet into the mound with a height of eight feet. In this gallery more than thirty skeletons were found. The skulls of some were missing, suggesting their removal for magical purposes, possibly to the temple for the rites of life through death. But the main point is the grouped relationship of this tomb of many burials – typical of the spread of the Great Goddess religion all along its maritime course from the Mediterranean – with the temple of Avebury, and the correlation of datable pottery from the two sites.

That morning I had stood at Stonehenge and been conscious of the ruins of a prehistoric 'city' around me. Now, in the South Circle at Avebury, I knew I was at the heart of the first metropolis to exist in Britain; for the floruit of Avebury was earlier than that of Stonehenge. It is this transfer of power from Avebury to Stonehenge that is still one of the historical secrets of Britain; we will know more as the search goes on. The transfer may have happened gradually during a span of years, or in a span of months, or perhaps dramatically in a single day or hour.

The chambers of the West Kennet Long Barrow were finally

sealed by the blocking of the entrance at a time in the ascendancy of the Beaker Cultures. This deliberate act seems to favour a possibility of events happening suddenly; a possibility that the immemorial power of the Great Goddess was swept aside in circumstances of intrigue, decisive action and the highest drama.

What is clear is that the heroes buried in their hundreds around Stonehenge led Britain forward into a new skyward-looking age, leaving Avebury, with its dark charnel chambers of Mother Earth, as now the second 'city', overlooked by the tombs of such comparatively few Wessex Culture chieftains in their round barrows whose lives had continued to centre on the old temple. The axe-carvings and Great Goddess symbol at Stonehenge seem to tell of religious revolution. The change of power from the temple of the Great Goddess at Avebury to the sky god temple of Stonehenge seems to tell the same story.

But Avebury was no mean city in its time. An enclosure in its confines a mile to the north-west on Windmill Hill, with evidence of great feasts in the massed quantities of animal bones in its ditches, has yielded eighteen stone implements, mainly axes, of the Neolithic form. Expert examination of the geological nature of these has revealed that they had been borne by man from as far away as western Cornwall, Great Langdale in Westmorland, and Caernarvonshire. There is one of spotted dolerite as well from the square mile on the summit of Mount Prescelly that provided the bluestones of Stonehenge. So the sacred mountain is linked also to Avebury, the second 'city' of Stonehenge Britain.

Leaving the stone implements aside, analysis of the composition of the pottery has revealed some containing powdered granite from Dartmoor, and fragments from other distant places. Dr Smith has written, '. . . the imported goods bear undeniable witness to the metropolitan character of the Avebury region in Late Neolithic times'.[4] Nowhere, not even at Stonehenge, is there such a concentration of 'foreign' stone implements. It is clear that in its day Avebury was the capital – religious, cultural, and commercial – of most of southern Britain. Then gradually and deliberately, or perhaps suddenly from a palace revolution or even battle, the capital was changed to Stonehenge, which was in any case better placed on the natural metal routes of trade, and which then triumphantly fanfared the outcome of the religious revolution with the new dawn-facing temple. Avebury then declined to the second 'city' in the land.

I left Avebury by the north entrance causeway as people have done for four thousand years. I drove along the Icknield Way, with the big lemon-curd moon seeming to ride along the Ridge Way high on my right and parallel with me like a target figure moving across a shooting-gallery. Every now and then the moon would pass behind a beech clump and its light would abruptly switch off and on. For mile after mile, the eight and nine hundred foot chalk escarpment rose black on my right.

On impulse, I stopped the car on the Icknield Way at the foot of White Horse Hill near Uffington, in Berkshire, and got out. The moon now sailed high and small – silver, shining. The near silence of the downs always makes sound analysis interesting – perhaps there is just a distant plane or tractor. On this still, cold night there was no sound, until a dog barked far away.

I looked up at the black silhouette of the chalk headland with its enigmatic Celtic figure of a stylised horse. Such horse symbols represented many of the Celts' fertility goddesses, such as Macha in Ireland and Rhiannon in Wales, and it may be that the great figure presiding above me in the moonlit night was first mothered by the Great Goddess of the Mediterranean. As I thought of the day I had spent among the ruins of the sacred cities of barbarian Britain, my standing, by chance, below the White Horse of Uffington seemed not inappropriate.

REFERENCES

1. Ashbee, Paul, *The Bronze Age Round Barrow in Britain*, Phoenix House, 1960.

2. Stone, J. F. S., *Wessex*, Thames and Hudson, 1958.

3. Graves, Robert, *The Greek Myths*, Penguin, 1955.

4. Smith, I. F., *Windmill Hill and Avebury*, Oxford University Press, 1965.

CHAPTER 6

Religion from the Mediterranean

IS IT just coincidence that a religious revolution similar to that suggested by archaeology in Britain was put into words in the myths of Greece? It does not appear to be so. All the evidence points to this religious revolution sweeping right across Europe.

The earliest idols of man known to archaeology are those of goddesses. Mr Robert Graves has written, 'Ancient Europe had no gods. The Great Goddess was regarded as immortal, changeless, and omnipotent, and the concept of fatherhood had not been introduced into religious thought.'[1]

The dramatic event that changed this matriarchal concept in Greece (the invasion of Greek-speaking Greeks) is described in the following myth. Apollo, the son of Zeus, left the island of Delos soon after his birth and went straight to Delphi, where he slew Python in the sacred shrine of the Oracle of Mother Earth. Apollo then took over the Oracle at Delphi, but retained the services of the Pythoness, the priestess, who had formerly been in the service of Mother Earth.

This describes in mythological language precisely the type of religious revolution, followed by compromise, visualised by Professor Atkinson from the archaeological evidence at Stonehenge. Apollo, the Sky Archer, is a typical form of god of the Indo-Europeans; and the Goddess Mother Earth, symbolised by the earth-wriggling snake, the Python, is equally representative of the till-then indigenous religions of the Mediterranean.

The archaeological evidence of the religion of the Great Goddess is particularly clear in Crete, with figurines of priestesses holding up snake-entwisted arms, and seal-stones carved with scenes of dominant female figures being saluted by male figures. The tombs in Crete tell the same story, with multiple burials associated with pottery vessels indicating offerings to the dead, typical of the religion of the Great Goddess in its spread through western and northern Europe. In Europe the fundamental impulse for this religion seems to have come from Crete, which was the focus of the early Aegean civilisation revealed in Troy, Cyprus, the islands of the Cyclades, and the Greek mainland.

Crete had a civilisation which extended back into the mists of the third millennium BC – an advanced civilisation which rivalled ancient Egypt itself. There were gracious royal palaces, several storeys high, adorned in beautiful, naturalistic Cretan art. Frescoes show the ladies of Crete so vivacious and chic in their clothes and hair styles that they have been christened aptly 'Les Parisiennes'. Common art motifs are flowers – in a pleasing natural style, full of life, which flows very differently from the stiffness of Egyptian art – and the life of the sea, octopuses and dolphins. The palaces, such as that at Knossos, had large ranges of storerooms, the accumulated wealth in which was inventoried on clay tablets in a script which we now call Linear A. It could be said that the clue to this wealth lay partly in their artistic dolphins, for the Cretans – or Minoans as Sir Arthur Evans, the discoverer of this lost civilisation, called them after their mythical king, King Minos – were a people of the sea. There is considerable evidence of direct Cretan sea-trade around the eastern Mediterranean back into the earlier part of the third millennium BC.

R. W. Hutchinson of Cambridge University has written, 'Cretan industries . . . must have depended very largely on imported materials. Gold, silver, tin, and lead all had to come by ships, and the island sources of copper must have been very inadequate for its needs'.[2] The need of these metals was great to satisfy this luxurious civilisation, and trade by sea-going ships was the only way to supply it.

The seals provide the best evidence of Cretan (or Minoan) ships. Very large numbers of these seals have been found in Crete. They were most commonly small stones of steatite (soap-stone) worked with summary but expressive designs of Minoan life, which were employed as a signet ring would be today. The seals show that by at least 2000 BC the Minoans had large sea-going vessels, equipped with a mast and sail, and powered also by oars. There are indications that the sail could be trimmed to some extent in a similar manner to an Arab lateen sail of the present day, to make use of varying wind directions to maintain the intended course. A vessel with forty oars is shown on a vase from an island in the Aegean, and it is probable that the pentekontor, the fifty-oared warship, was first used before 1500 BC. By comparison, the astonishing voyaging of the Vikings was done in vessels which had an average of twenty oars, so, at least, we know that there was no limit on the maritime potential of the Cretans from the oar-power of their vessels.

Some vessels are shown with a form of deck-cabin, and there are other indications that some cargo-ships may have been decked. Most vessels had an exceptionally high prow mounted with a figure-head. Estimates have been made that these vessels could have run to a length of over ninety feet. Harbours and dry-docks have been identified in Crete from this Minoan period, indicating the habitual nature of this trade carried in sea-going ships.

The dropping of this pebble of luxurious, maritime civilisation off the coast of south-eastern Europe caused ripples that spread out eventually to barbarian Ireland and Britain. These are the cultural left arm of the 'pincer movement' on Britain, which I referred to in the last chapter. It was a chain reaction round the coasts of Europe, initiated by the demand of luxurious Crete for metals, and carried on by prospectors, traders, colonists, and adventurous seamen.

Geoffrey Bibby of the Aarhus Museum, Denmark, says of these people, 'They were part traders and part prospectors, these wide-ranging sea captains. But though they scarcely realised it, they were most to make their mark as missionaries.'[3]

The present archaeological evidence points to the existence of Cretan trading colonies in south-east Italy, Malta, Sicily and Sardinia, and these colonies led to the great settlement at Los Millares, in south-east Spain, the greatest centre of Aegean influence in the western Mediterranean. From here the metals from the vast resources of Spain were embarked for Crete.

Some ships sailed further on still into the Atlantic (Bibby sees the entire voyages to the British Isles carried out in Cretan ships) and up the west European coast to Brittany and thence to Ireland and Britain. Whether this trading along three thousand miles of coast was done in individual ships or by trading between intermediate ports is an open question (perhaps both played a part), but the fact remains that an archaeological chain links all these places together around the coast of Europe. The chain is the religion of the Great Goddess which the traders took with them and established in all the places I have mentioned along this route. Los Millares in Spain revitalised the religion on its way; and from here to the British Isles it is especially revealed in the practice of collective burial, in the architecture of the tombs, and in the magical symbols carved on the stones of the tombs. The Aegean settlement at Los Millares in Spain is the great stepping-stone between Crete and the British Isles.

When one thinks of the variations in the rituals and conceptions of Christianity in its spread, it would be unwise to expect the Great Goddess religion to manifest itself in exactly similar terms throughout this great distance, and it is possible that even her name (which we do not know) may not have been the same everywhere. But the concept appears to have been carried of a goddess of life and death, who conferred the most fervent wish of man, immortality, and the evidence is that here was perhaps the earliest religion of Europe to spread over a vast area in a reasonably codified form.

To deal with the related form of tomb architecture first: some collective burial in Crete took place in 'tholoi', which were bee-hive-shaped tombs, with corbelled, or inward overlapping, courses of stone working up to the apex of the roof. The idea of this corbelled roof was also used at Los Millares and thence to one of the greatest prehistoric tombs of northern Europe, New Grange, which is situated twenty miles or so north of Dublin near the River Boyne. The 'tholoi' in the Aegean were approached by a 'dromos' or long entrance passage cut into the slope of the hillside, and this feature is paralleled by a long covered passage leading into the burial chambers at Los Millares and New Grange, causing the two latter to be known to archaeologists as Passage Graves, which is the name applied, also, to the hundreds of tombs of similar architecture in western Europe and the British Isles. So closely allied is the architectural tomb form of New Grange in Ireland, Los Millares in Spain, and Crete that, if it were not for the sake of archaeological clarity, the term 'tholos' could be applied to them all.

New Grange and Los Millares both exhibit two inter-related systems of construction. One is the use of megaliths, which simply means large stones. In this system of architecture entire walls and roofs of chambers are supplied by single stone slabs weighing many tons. Often backing these for stability and support, or in filling spaces between the slabs, is unmortared walling formed of smaller stones, and this is called cyclopean walling. The use of the large stone slab technique is the more characteristic of these tombs generally, and so archaeologists refer to these structures as megalithic tombs, and their builders, in general, as Megalith Builders.

Scientific dating methods are revealing that variations of these megalithic collective burial tombs were built in north-west Europe for at least two thousand years, in very approximate figures, from before 3000 BC to 1000 BC, and we can visualise some variation of the worship of the Great Goddess taking place at them during this period.

The burial chambers of Los Millares under their round mounds sometimes contained more than a hundred burials. Near by, the town – perhaps the first actual town in western Europe – circled by a great bastioned wall and covering thirteen acres, had a cistern and ducted water supply, and rectangular stone houses. The archaeological evidence suggests that this was a colony of Cretan or Aegean people at Los Millares, and Dr Glyn Daniel of Cambridge University, who is familiar to the general public on television in the series 'Animal, Vegetable or Mineral' and 'Man Discovers His Past', suggests a tentative date for this settlement having first been established between 3500–2700 BC.

Dr Glyn Daniel has made a particular study of the spread of these megalith tombs in west and north-west Europe, and he writes in collaboration with Professor Sean P. Ó Ríordáin:

> 'We see New Grange, and the other Passage Graves of the British Isles as tombs (and perhaps also cult shrines and temples) of important chiefs of prospecting and trading communities who came from Iberia first of all in the end of the fourth millennium BC and who traded and voyaged backwards and forwards along the Atlantic seaways for fifteen hundred years or more, and as a direct result of whose voyages of exploration and trade there eventually developed the metallurgical industry of Ireland at the end of the third millennium BC.'[4]

Dr Daniel suggests a tentative date for the New Grange tomb of around 2500 BC. There is a scientific dating by the radio-carbon method for the similar Passage Grave, the Mound of the Hostages at Tara, of around 2100 BC.

What does New Grange itself reveal of the people who built it? The mound is now forty feet high, 280 feet in diameter and covers about an acre. The entrance passage and chambering lead about eighty feet into the mound and the height rises to nineteen feet six inches to the magnificent corbelled roof over the central chamber deep in the mound. A considerable amount of the stonework has been very carefully dressed to shape. It is the centre of an area of monuments in the Bend of the Boyne showing similar impressive features.

Just as Stonehenge indicates a large, organised population in Britain for its building, so New Grange shows a powerful society in Ireland. A society moreover deriving its skills and knowledge from Los Millares and not very greatly removed from the civilisations of the Aegean. Dr Daniel writes of New Grange, '. . . as we stand outside the great tomb . . . we must . . . sense that we are in the very middle of one of the great centres of Iberian or possibly Aegean settlement in ancient times'.[5]

Once again the former concept of lone savages, remote from any civilising influence, scratching an existence from nature in the British Isles of four and five thousand years ago is shown obviously to be incorrect. The settlements of the maritime spread of the Megalith Builders with their Great Goddess were great communities, perhaps even to be compared in organisation and power with the latter zenith at the time of Stonehenge in the region of 1500 BC. We have seen with the Great Goddess symbol carved at Stonehenge that the New Grange society was one of the threads leading in some way ancestrally from the west into the monument on Salisbury Plain. This is an abstract way of saying that a swarthy faced Mediterranean captain stationed by the steersman peered anxiously ahead past the towering prow of his ship as it nosed slowly forward to the rhythmical creak and thud of the oars being rowed at half power up the narrowing, unknown treachery of the Bristol Channel. He knew what lay behind in Ireland, but soon he would find what lay ahead in the land of Wessex.

Architecture apart, the trail leads back from Stonehenge and the Goddess symbol, to Brittany, Los Millares, and the Aegean by what is called megalithic art; that is, the religious symbols carved on the walls and ceilings of the tombs, and also on idols associated with the tombs. The Great Goddess was symbolised in the Aegean at this period by stylised idols variously emphasising her eyes, necklace, breasts, and a number of patterns on her clothing such as lozenges and chevrons. These and other magical art motifs of the Great Goddess spread right round Europe into the British Isles. At least forty-five of the stones of New Grange, for instance, bear her symbols. Of these, the finely carved stone at the entrance to the passage at New Grange, showing spiral patterns indicating the eyes of the Goddess, bears a notable resemblance to the carving on the stone at the entrance to the holiest sanctum in the refined architecture of Hal Tarxien, the neolithic temple on Malta.

As one gazes at these designs carved in the stones of the tombs of Ireland and Brittany, one's mind tries to grapple with the tremendous cryptic message in them in terms of living people. Just to see one is to see a slab of stone covered with meaningless doodlings. To see hundreds in the countryside of Brittany and on desolate hills in Ireland like Loughcrew, covered with the repetitive motifs of concentric circles, spirals, 'snakes', chevrons, and lozenges sets the mind struggling to get to the heart of their meaning. Religion and magic are carved there clearly enough, but the mind inevitably strives after the thoughts of the carvers. The naturalistic art of 20,000 years ago in the painted caves of France is evocative, but the mind can become deeply tantalised by the patterned art of the Megalith Builders of 5,000 years ago. Professor O'Kelly of Cork University remarked to me, 'Do not become too mentally involved with it. It has driven some people mad.'

Strangely, that enormous megalithic tomb, the West Kennet Long Barrow, which I described in the Avebury complex of ruins, is undecorated. Dr Daniel sees the West Kennet Long Barrow and the other similar tombs grouped towards the Severn–Cotswold region as perhaps representing 'a latter-day Passage Grave people'. Fashion may have changed regarding decoration. The cult of the Mother Goddess is clear enough in the practice of collective burial and the megalithic architecture of the tomb in spite of the absence of this art. So we see one of the end flowerings of this religion at Avebury on a remote island in the Atlantic, the religion having been started on its way by the Cretans in their ships searching for metals.

The recent excavation at Wayland's Smithy, the long barrow in Berkshire, by Professors Piggott and Atkinson seems to show the arrival of the megalithic cult there. An earlier, small long barrow enclosing a timber chamber with about fourteen burials in it was overlaid within a period of one generation around 2800 BC by a much larger long barrow with sarsen chambering, in general similar in design to the West Kennet Long Barrow.

What do we know of the Great Goddess religion? Some later

myths, such as that of Aphrodite and Adonis which we have mentioned – the all-powerful goddess and young annually-dying-and-resurrecting vegetation god – probably throw light on the subject. It is thought that the dark charnel chambers reveal a concept of life and death taking place in the earthy womb of the Goddess and that she could be invoked in her underworld through ritual pits, which are found in association with collective tombs and at Avebury and Stonehenge. Myth lends support to this Underworld conception with the chasm of Mother Earth at Delphi. It is possible that oracular powers played a specific part in the religion generally. The Great Goddess no doubt exerted omnipotence over the fertility of crops and herds. The exaggerated massiveness and indestructibility of megalithic tombs suggests a conferring of immortality by the Goddess, which the tombs would protect in the same way that the Pyramids are known to have been built to guard by their permanence the immortal after-life of the Egyptian kings. It is possible that it was this offer of immortality in the form of a specific religion under an omnipotent goddess that led to the wide spread of the religion. It seems certain that this religion existed for a longer period than has Christianity in the British Isles, to be finally subjugated but not abandoned on the arrival of the sky gods of war.

The Minoans must have thought that their all-powerful Goddess, who protected them in war and peace, life and death would rule for eternity, but the Indo-European Mycenaeans are thought to have conquered Crete around 1500 BC and the Great Goddess dwindled into subsidiary forms of fertility goddesses, such as Aphrodite under the aegis of Zeus, by the time of the Trojan War.

By brilliant scholarship, Michael Ventris and John Chadwick deciphered the script on the tablets in the storerooms of the Minoan and Mycenaean palaces of this later period around 1400 BC. This script is known as Linear B, and is later than the Minoan Linear A script which is still undeciphered. Some of the Linear B tablets recount offerings to deities, one of these being Potnia; in English, the Mistress. John Chadwick writes, 'We know from Minoan and Mycenaean monuments that a female deity played a prominent part in their religion, and I have therefore suggested identifying Potnia with this figure.'[6] The simple transcendent title, the Mistress, translatable into any language, is an enticing name for the unknown Great Goddess whose cult spread around Europe. Fascinating as this possibility is, it can be no more than speculation. But Potnia could be equated with a common Minoan symbol of a goddess standing on a mountain or pillar with two lion supporters. This raises parallels with the goddess Artemis of the later Greeks or Diana of the Romans, expressing mankind's supremacy over the world of animals, and with undertones similar to those of the Aphrodite and Adonis myth betokening the sacrifice of young males for fertility purposes. In the present state of knowledge one can only parade points such as these from the myths, archaeology, and writings of Crete and Greece that do seem to have possible relevance to the Great Goddess. The search goes on.

In Britain, the Goddess possibly lost her immemorial power by about 1600 BC. Here the clash of religions was probably paralleled by a clash of races, as the skeletons in the chambered tombs of the Great Goddess are predominantly those of long-headed, small-featured, lightly built people of Mediterranean type, and those in the individual, warrior, round barrow graves are round-headed, heavily featured of the north European type. Out of this religious and racial fusion came the brilliance of the Stonehenge period, with the Indo-Europeans, as always, dominating society.

The people of Mediterranean ancestry after this fusion formed the common stock of the population of Britain and probably still clung as far as they could to their goddess of fertility whose help they needed more than ever in their reduced condition. War gods were not for them; their prayers were that the corn would grow and the sow farrow next spring, or they would die.

The cult of fertility persisted for poorer people. In the Middle Ages the Christian Church was bitterly opposed to the continuing practice of pagan, orgiastic rites, which probably had their roots in the Great Goddess. At Avebury, a surgeon-barber was crushed under one of the huge stones that had been felled, probably in a concerted attempt to destroy the pagan temple. A Christian church was built there, causing a strange antagonistic continuity of sanctity. At Knowlton in Dorset, a twelfth-century church, now deserted, is sited in the centre of a temple similar to Avebury, which we will go to later.

The leading figures of the major religions of the present day are male – the Christian God, Jehovah, Mohammed, Buddha. A time seems to have come in the development of the social power of man when he turned from the Mother Goddess – the comforter and begetter, terrible though her form could be sometimes – to male deities. It was as if the umbilical cord of mankind was cut. The timing of the building of Stonehenge seems like a paean celebrating this severance in Britain. But could it be dangerous to stray too far from the earthy essentials of the Mother Goddess?

It is surprising that even scientists are talking more and more of 'mastery of nature'. Matter is indestructible and man cannot change the laws of the universe; it is there, with man a part of it, adapting to it – in the Darwinian sense – if he is wise, as his knowledge of it increases. The juxtaposing of elements for such things as tools and medicaments is understanding not mastery. Man cannot master nature unless he becomes god, but he has made god in his image. The god of the universe is universal and anthropomorphosis seems the essential misconception; if it is necessary, all-embracing Mother is a simple and satisfactory symbol.

REFERENCES

1. Graves, Robert, *The Greek Myths*, Penguin, 1955.

2. Hutchinson, R. W., *Prehistoric Crete*, Penguin, 1962.

3. Bibby, Geoffrey, *Four Thousand Years Ago*, Collins, 1961.

4. Ó Ríordáin, S. P. and Daniel, Glyn, *New Grange and the Bend of the Boyne*, Thames and Hudson, 1965.

5. Ó Ríordáin, S. P. and Daniel, Glyn, *op. cit.*

6. Chadwick, John, *The Decipherment of Linear B*, Cambridge University Press, 1958.

CHAPTER 7

The Wessex Culture

KNOWLEDGE OF prehistory must be based on archaeology. Myths without an archaeological foundation to build on remain stories unrelated to any specific period of man's history. Broadly, the Victorians viewed archaeology as a static pastime. Sites were dug into and the finds treated as collectors' curios; lack of knowledge adding to their mysterious aura. In their assurance of human progress no urgency attached to the study of the past. Theorising and controversy rang the changes with what little archaeological evidence there was and a mass of largely irrelevant documentary material.

Now archaeology is very similarly placed to say nuclear physics or astronomy. Intensive research by excavation is producing facts that are built into a frame of genuine knowledge of prehistoric man; knowledge that a short time ago was utterly non-existent. It is as if man was recovering from amnesia (which is a dangerous state), and was slowly piecing together his past life.

So far in this book I have made general references to several cultures such as the Beaker Cultures and the Wessex Culture in prehistoric Britain. In the absence of documentary history, which gives information such as tribal names and the spread and conquests of peoples, archaeologists attempt to remedy this lack by the study of the tangible objects early man has left after him. Where these objects from two different archaeological sites resemble each other, the communities which made them are said to belong to the same culture. Frequently these two communities will have emerged from a common background of race, religion, social custom and organisation. The cultural affinity of the two communities may mean that they were linked politically, under the same king for instance, but this is far from inevitable. Pottery is the main evidence used by archaeologists in the distinguishing of cultures. The marking of sometimes relatively closely datable material of the same culture wherever found on maps, known as distribution maps, produces evidence of the spreading and waxing and waning of cultures. Such things as trade, conquests and technological advances are revealed with reasonable clarity.

The period of cultural build-up and fusion producing the zenith of the Stonehenge period appears to start shortly before 3000 BC in Britain. Prior to this the island was sparsely inhabited by food-hunting and gathering savages who did not know any farming techniques of seed-sowing or animal domestication. Radio-carbon dating has revealed that about this time, people of ultimately Mediterranean origin who were farmers and pottery-makers entered Britain in the south-west and spread eastward. These people are named by archaeologists as the Windmill Hill culture, after the enclosure built by them on Windmill Hill near Avebury, which I referred to on page 43. The Windmill Hill culture buried their dead collectively in long barrows. They cultivated wheat and barley, and had domesticated animals, mainly cattle. They had no knowledge of metals, so, with their farming and pottery-making, are defined as neolithic, literally belonging to the New Stone Age, distinguishing them from earlier Stone Ages. The descendants of these first farmers in Britain appear to form the common stock of the population right down to the period we are interested in when the final architectural building of Stonehenge took place, around 1500 BC.

Somewhere, towards 2000 BC (it is thought in the present state of knowledge) another culture appears – the Rinyo-Clacton Culture. This strange name is made up by the linking of two Rinyo-Clacton sites – Rinyo, on the island of Ronsay in the Orkneys, and Clacton on the Essex coast at the other extreme of Britain.

The interpretation of the social significance of the Rinyo-Clacton Culture and how it arose in Britain is one of the major archaeological problems at the present time. That it had great social significance is clear from the fact that Rinyo-Clacton pottery has been found in considerable quantity at Woodhenge and its neighbouring area, and also at most of the Avebury group of monuments, including the West Kennet Long Barrow. Stonehenge, itself, revealed Rinyo-Clacton pottery from the time when the original 'henge' monument was constructed. This culture's funeral rite was one of cremation, and some of the burials were in 'henges'. Unfortunately the

Rinyo-Clacton Culture did not customarily place grave-goods with its dead, so one of the most fruitful sources of information to archaeologists is lacking. It is these Rinyo-Clacton people that Dr I. F. Smith considers were the builders of Avebury in conjunction with the descendants of the Windmill Hill people.

Because of a comparatively recent recognition of the importance of the Rinyo-Clacton people, they remain at the present time tantalisingly elusive. All one can do is bring forward certain points about them. That they had some seafaring ability is shown by the finding of their amazingly preserved stone-built houses notably at Skara Brae and also of course at Rinyo on the remote Orkneys. Dr J. F. S. Stone wrote in 1958 that some of the pottery '. . . may be derived from Late Neolithic styles in north-western France and Iberia'.[1] One fragment of pottery from the Orkney sites is decorated with the unmistakable eye-like spirals and lozenges of the art of the tombs of the Megalith Builders. To erect any hypothesis on the strength of one sherd of pottery would be unwise, but it may be significant that pottery that seems related to Rinyo-Clacton has been found at the great Passage Grave tomb, New Grange, in Ireland, which I have described.

What has emerged fairly clearly in recent years is that the Rinyo-Clacton people, far from being wandering bands of pedlars living at low subsistence level, as was previously thought, were a people of considerable ability and organisation and possibly provided leadership for the common stock of Windmill Hill ancestry.

There is no evidence that they had knowledge of metals, but this may not present a true picture as the lack of grave-goods in their burials makes this point more difficult to determine. But on the strength of this they are classed as a Late Neolithic people.

On to this scene erupted soon after 2000 BC people of quite a different culture from the Rhineland. These were the Bell-Beaker people whose single burials, which were not cremated, were accompanied by a pot shaped like a bell. These people had fine archery equipment, and sometimes copper daggers and gold ornaments. The distribution pattern of their spread over western Europe suggests that they were a great trading people of restless energy and determination.

Soon after they were followed into Britain by the Corded-Ware-Battle-Axe Culture. These were the people who spread quickly from the southern Russian steppes, and who appear to be of Indo-European origin. These battle-axe users mingled with the Bell-Beaker folk in Britain to produce the Necked Beaker Culture, so called from a rather Scotch-thistle-head shape of their funeral pots. The warrior tradition is clear from the start of Necked Beaker burials in Britain. Finely carved stone battle-axes and large well designed daggers of true bronze, not copper, accompany the dead. They were buried under large round barrows, and this tradition accounts for many of the barrows around Stonehenge and elsewhere. Beaker pottery has been found in later archaeological layers at many of the henge monuments. Broadly then, as far as southern England is concerned, these are the cultures that concern us before the final floruit of Stonehenge – the Windmill Hill and its descendants, the Rinyo-Clacton, the Bell-Beaker, and the Necked Beaker.

It is these that rapidly, in the perspective of human progress, led up to an extraordinary period lasting for about two centuries, from 1600–1400 BC, in the affairs of the people of Britain. The culture that dominated these two centuries was named by Professor Stuart Piggott in 1937 the Wessex Culture. Like Stonehenge itself, with which it is associated, the Wessex Culture is a unique phenomenon in Britain. It is a culture related to status and wealth, by which it is separated from the evidence of other cultures coexisting with it. It is the culture not of a whole community or communities, but solely of the aristocrats of the period, the evidence of whom has been found in only between 100 and 130 graves. Who were these aristocrats; where did they come from? This is not yet clear. It is possible that they were a development in a period of success from their predecessors; that they resulted from fusion of the preceding cultures with the Necked Beaker Culture dominant, and certainly there is evidence of this latter culture overlapping into the Wessex Culture period down to 1550 BC.

On the other hand, it is the exotic features of the Wessex Culture that are so striking, and it may be that here there is evidence of war-lords arriving in Britain from overseas and setting up dynasties that ruled such areas as Wessex, Cornwall and Norfolk. The Wessex Culture has no one burial or group of burials that compares with those of Mycenae in magnificence, but the Wessex graves have their own characteristic splendour making them outstanding in northern Europe. Sir Richard Colt Hoare and William Cunnington worked together in the early nineteenth century to unearth an assemblage of truly remarkable possessions of the Early Bronze Age royalty and aristocracy of Wessex. This collection is now impressively displayed at the Museum, Devizes, Wiltshire, giving this small museum critical importance to the student of barbarian Europe.

Any lay preconception that the capabilities and knowledge of Stonehenge man were very limited must be swept away confronted by this proof of the skill of Bronze Age miners, metallurgists and smiths. By that time in Britain, men of specialised knowledge could recognise ore-bearing rocks, smelt them, if necessary, as in the case of bronze, alloy the resultant metals, and cast, beat, and decorate fine things. Most of the weapons of the Wessex Culture are of true bronze, analysis having shown proportions near to the ideal of 90 per cent copper and 10 per cent tin. Such an alloy would not occur by chance. It has properties for weapons excelling that of some mild steels.

The fine weapons and metal ornaments were the products of industries native to north-west Europe and not exported from the advanced civilisations of the Mediterranean. This is clearly shown by distribution maps of metal goods of characteristic native design and the finding of such things as casting moulds in north-west Europe.

Metal objects first begin to appear in Britain around 1800 BC. That by 1600 BC onwards, an outstanding concentration of them should occur in Wessex can only be the sign of the social dominance of the people there, as the metal ores lay at their nearest a hundred miles away, and in the case of gold across the sea in the Wicklow Mountains of Ireland. In these circumstances, the possession of one bronze dagger, with the implications involved by its presence in Wessex of labour, knowledge, skill, acquirement and transport demonstrates both wealth and power. The accoutrement of a knight of the Middle Ages evidencing his power in many channels of society is perhaps comparable. Colt Hoare alone uncovered at least twenty-two Wessex Culture dagger graves some of which had more than one dagger, as well as other graves with smaller knife-daggers.

The wealth accompanying Wessex Culture burials can best be shown by describing several of them. The striking panoply with the royal burial under Bush Barrow near Stonehenge has been mentioned earlier. Clandon Barrow near Dorchester, Dorset, has similar royal grave-goods as well as a solid amber cup. In the Golden Barrow at Upton Lovell on the west side of Salisbury Plain, a cremation was accompanied by a bronze dagger, a meticulously decorated rectangular gold plate about 6¼ inches long by 3 inches wide, thirteen cylindrical gold beads, two gold cones and a gold button, all imaginatively ornamented, and a magnificent amber necklace made up of several hundred beads inter-set with larger complexly designed and bored plates of the precious substance. Great Barrow in the same group covered a cremation with a necklace of amber, shale and faience beads.

Manton Barrow, four miles east of Avebury, contained an inhumation with an amber disc bound in gold, a gold bound bead, a composite pendant of gold and bronze in the form of a miniature halberd, an amber pommel for a dagger and a bronze knife-dagger with several other bronze objects.

Around Stonehenge, a bell-barrow in the Normanton group had gold bound amber discs and a halberd pendant similar to those in the Manton Barrow and also a gold button with other objects of gold and amber. Another bell-barrow in the outstanding Winterbourne Stoke group west of Stonehenge revealed a cremation in the remains of a wooden coffin with bronze fittings. This is one example of many Wessex Culture graves that have revealed signs of skilfully worked organic materials that have only left traces. As well as other coffin burials, Wessex graves have revealed traces of wooden sheaths for some of the numerous daggers, in one case at Normanton still retaining the refined detail of a sheath lining of cloth. These organic finds are fragmentary but there is no reason to suppose that their working was inferior to the metal goods. An interesting social aspect is revealed by a swan's bone from another Normanton barrow. This is broken and ravaged by time but appears to have been made into a flute. It was accompanied with a bronze dagger, knife-dagger, well-made whetstone, and a bronze dress-pin of central European design.

Not to continue at too great length, it can be seen that Wessex Culture graves show evidence which potentially could contribute to a clear concept of their society. The finery of an aristocratic class appears (perhaps both male and female), and this is often associated with the dagger of the warrior, as well as with his finely carved stone battle-axe as at Wilsford Down south of Stonehenge. The bronze axes, such as that in Bush Barrow, lend themselves more readily to an interpretation of weapons in the hands of a ruling class than to tools for menial work.

The widespread contact of Wessex societies with other wealthy societies in Europe is apparent. There have been found in Wessex faience beads from the Mediterranean, bronze dress-pins from central Europe, amber from Denmark, gold from Ireland. The pottery shows links with many distant societies. Wessex daggers of straight-sided form are identical with many in the dagger graves of Brittany, and Breton daggers have gold pin decoration like that in Bush Barrow. The Wessex tradition of working in thin sheet gold resembles that at Mycenae. Is all this evidence of trade, or a spread of fashion and ideas, pillage, gift-giving? We will discuss this later.

Stonehenge, the finest building of barbarian Europe, is a Wessex Culture monument. This great structure and the wealth of its builders implies a momentous period in the history of Britain, a period that archaeology is slowly revealing.

How else does the Wessex Culture evidence itself? Perhaps most obviously in the specialised shape of its barrows. Firstly, the bell-barrow, which has a large mound surrounded by a level area bounded by a circular ditch, giving a profile shape to the barrow rather like a bell. These usually contain male warrior burials. Secondly, the disc-barrow, which is a flat area bounded by a circular ditch with a bank outside. In the central flat area are usually one or more quite small mounds with the cremation of a female under it. Both these types of barrow are usually large – the bell frequently eight feet or considerably more in height, and the disc up to seventy yards or more in diameter.

The earlier Wessex Culture burials are inhumations, possibly showing influence in the first fusion of the Beaker Cultures, who inhumed their dead, but later the Wessex Culture rite was cremation, the burnt bones being placed in large urns, of various diagnostic types, which were placed upside down in the grave and the barrow erected over them. It is not necessary to go into further detail but it may be said that most rich burials revealing bronze weapons, and implements, sceptres, amber, gold, jet and Kimmeridge shale (in the form of ornaments and sometimes cups) and Mediterranean faience beads, in the British Bronze Age, are those of the Wessex Culture.

I have said that these cluster most thickly around Stonehenge itself, and less so around Avebury. Where else shall we find them? Let us go out into Britain and explore for the Wessex Culture; in other words, to put it in more human terms, for places where the heroes of Stonehenge Britain lived and died.

REFERENCE

1. Stone, J. F. S., *Wessex*, Thames and Hudson, 1958.

CHAPTER 8

The Five 'Cities' of Stonehenge Wessex

I WAS looking at a distribution map of the Bronze Age in Mr L. V. Grinsell's book, *The Archaeology of Wessex*, which was published in 1958. In the key to the map was printed, 'Wessex Culture Barrows' with a symbol for bell-barrows and one for disc-barrows. Then under, it said, 'Group, with both types'.[1] These large collections of Wessex Culture barrows were symbolised by a bold black dot enclosed by a circle.

Raising my eyes to the map itself, five clusters of these bold black dots stood out from the page, running north-eastward up the chalk downs from, first, near the coast at Poor Lot by Dorchester in Dorset to the next at Oakley Down also in Dorset on Cranborne Chase; then on to the greatest cluster around Stonehenge, with a sort of antenna stretching north in the direction of Avebury. From the bold eye-catching symbols around Avebury on the Marlborough Downs, my eye travelled to the fifth and last symbol marked near Lambourn on the Berkshire Downs.

Four of these groups have one or more henge monuments in their general district, namely Poor Lot, Oakley Down, Stonehenge and Avebury. No henge monument has been found near Lambourn.

In my opinion these are the five great communities of Stonehenge Wessex; all on chalk downs, as one might expect, with safe open grazing, dry to live and travel on, and easy to till. At them all, water was almost on the doorstep, as it were, or in a near-by valley for the lowly to fetch. I have focused attention on the Dorset coastal region by mentioning the Poor Lot barrow collection, but impressive as this is, it merely high-lights what must have been an area of great population and power, a kingdom probably, lying on a great chalk ridge for ten miles or so between Dorchester and the coast. This community lying in the hinterland behind the natural harbour at Weymouth could very conceivably be the greatest coastal trading society in Stonehenge Britain. Certainly the wealth indicated by the archaeological material found here would support this possibility. This wealth has been found in the barrows of the royalty and aristocracy that ruled it.

When you leave the race-track-like road joining Dorchester to Bridport and walk steeply up on to the lark-serenaded downs at Poor Lot you reach a collection of over forty barrows. Seven of these are bell-barrows and six disc-barrows. The setting is magnificent – to the south, the sea lies hundreds of feet below, down great smooth curves of turf, and all round the enormous domes of chalk are divided by deep, wooded valleys.

For ten miles from Poor Lot eastward following the Ridge Way along the crest of the downs parallel to the coast are some of the most impressive barrows in Britain. I have stood in Maiden Castle, the largest Celtic stronghold in Britain, which is to the north of this ridge, and from it counted seventeen enormous barrows almost at a glance, silhouetted on the skyline and strung along five miles or so of the down crest. They seemed infinitely ancient and enigmatic like silent watchers as I regarded them, and so they may have seemed to the pre-Roman Celts living in Maiden Castle, for to them they were a thousand years old.

Such of these barrows as have been excavated have produced a number of bronze daggers, one with a gold pommel-mount, and a bronze axe, similar to the carvings at Stonehenge, but perhaps the most significant aspect of this area near the harbour of Weymouth is the distant origin of these and other things found here. Stone axes from Cornwall and an urn of Cornish type show a definite link with this land of tin; a metal essential to Wessex for turning soft copper to unyielding bronze. Trade the other way through Weymouth may be revealed by the finding of two cups made of shale from Kimmeridge on the Dorset coast in barrows near Honiton in Devon.

Trade links with Brittany are shown by a Breton four-handled vase found on Portland Bill by Weymouth, and by a hoard of Breton axes in a barrow near Eggardon in the area. A stone axe from the mountain known as Pike O'Stickle in the Lake District has been found on the chalk ridge, and of even greater interest from the point of view of trade implications, one from Antrim in Ireland, the land of gold. Some of these items can only have come by sea.

The burial of a man who may have ruled the province focused on this great trading port was found in a large barrow, twenty feet high, near Maiden Castle. Like Bush Barrow near Stonehenge, this burial in the Clandon Barrow, so called, seems clearly that of a king. As with the Stonehenge king, this king in Dorset had a finely decorated lozenge-shaped gold breastplate measuring 6 inches by 4½ inches, suggesting that this adornment was a symbol of monarchy. This supposition is again reinforced by the Clandon burial being accompanied by a sceptre-head of Kimmeridge shale with large gold studs inserted into it. A bronze dagger was also present but perhaps the most striking object from the point of view of wealth and trade was a large-handled cup of amber carved from a single nodule of the precious substance. The origin of the amber was probably Denmark, which supplied most of the wealthy centres of Europe, such as Mycenae, at that time, and through antiquity. Other Wessex Culture burials have had with them similar cups of amber and also Kimmeridge shale.

I have learnt from lecturing to people who are interested in history that it is a new thought to many of them that Stonehenge is not a monument standing in cultural isolation; that it is surrounded by the barrows, Woodhenge, the Cursus and so on, of its period. But here, in the Dorchester region of Dorset, forty-five miles from Stonehenge, there is a similar assemblage of monuments – including the Wessex Culture barrows, bell and disc – and from these have come similar cultural material, such as the bronze daggers, gold breastplates and pottery.

Apart from the similarity of barrow design and grave-goods, there are two of the problematical henge monuments, the enclosures with bank outside ditch, by Dorchester, relating in some way to such structures as Woodhenge, by Stonehenge. So, leaving aside the unique structure of Stonehenge itself, here in Dorset is an assemblage of monuments and cultural material which must indicate that similar sorts of people and societies must have coexisted at Stonehenge and Dorchester.

The significance of individual groups of barrows, such as that on Normanton Down near Stonehenge, covering perhaps half a mile, has always been obvious, but far less stressed has been the major assemblages of a number of such barrow groups with henges and sometimes cursuses; the assemblages dating in general to the second millennium BC, although the long barrows in them show roots going back a thousand years earlier.

To my mind, the recognition of these major assemblages of varied monuments in five specific areas of ruins through the chalklands of Wessex – Lambourn, Avebury, Stonehenge, Oakley and Dorchester – provides the most potentially fruitful attitude of research into the social life of Stonehenge man. Each assemblage should be regarded as the evidence of a social unit, and the detailed evidence from it related to the continuing evidence of life in it, through the second millennium BC. I would describe it as a sort of town-planning in reverse. Here is the opportunity to study the development of single communities over periods of centuries, rather than the diffused relating of individual cultures all over Britain; a digging of thought deep into one complete assemblage of ruins rather than the lateral spread of thought over great areas that may have now yielded most of the social evidence this line of research can reveal. I think that the map showing the five areas of Bronze Age ruins in Wessex is one of our most significant historical documents.

I have spent much time exploring the Bronze Age map of the Dorchester area; walking along its wonderful Ridge Way, free-standing in space, with the barrows at its side, its henges and barrow groups. I recently revisited the Museum in Dorchester and saw the regalia and weapons of the society that once lived in the area. I discussed the Bronze Age trade in Kimmeridge shale, a smooth, black substance from Kimmeridge Bay on the Dorset coast, with Mr R. N. R. Peers, the Museum archaeologist. This substance found its way all over Wessex in the form of carved, handled cups, beads, buttons and belt-sliders. We looked at the Museum model of Maumbury Rings, the henge on the outskirts of Dorchester. This showed the henge as it was when excavated – a strange sight. Arranged around inside its bank were forty-four narrow, tapering shafts, almost needle-like in profile, and about thirty-five feet deep. Again, the difference in design of individual henge monuments is revealed – an extraordinary aberration in this case. The great depth of the shafts recalls a symmetrical shaft under a pond-barrow near Stonehenge, excavated by Mr Paul Ashbee, which was a hundred feet deep with Bronze Age material in its fill including a very-well-made lime bast rope. I merely connect these two in terms of organised labour. Whatever the purpose of these two structures, Bronze Age man has left enough to show that he was skilled in many fields of endeavour.

I said good-bye to Mr Peers and went to Maumbury Rings on the outskirts of Dorchester. Standing in the circle, I tried to recapture

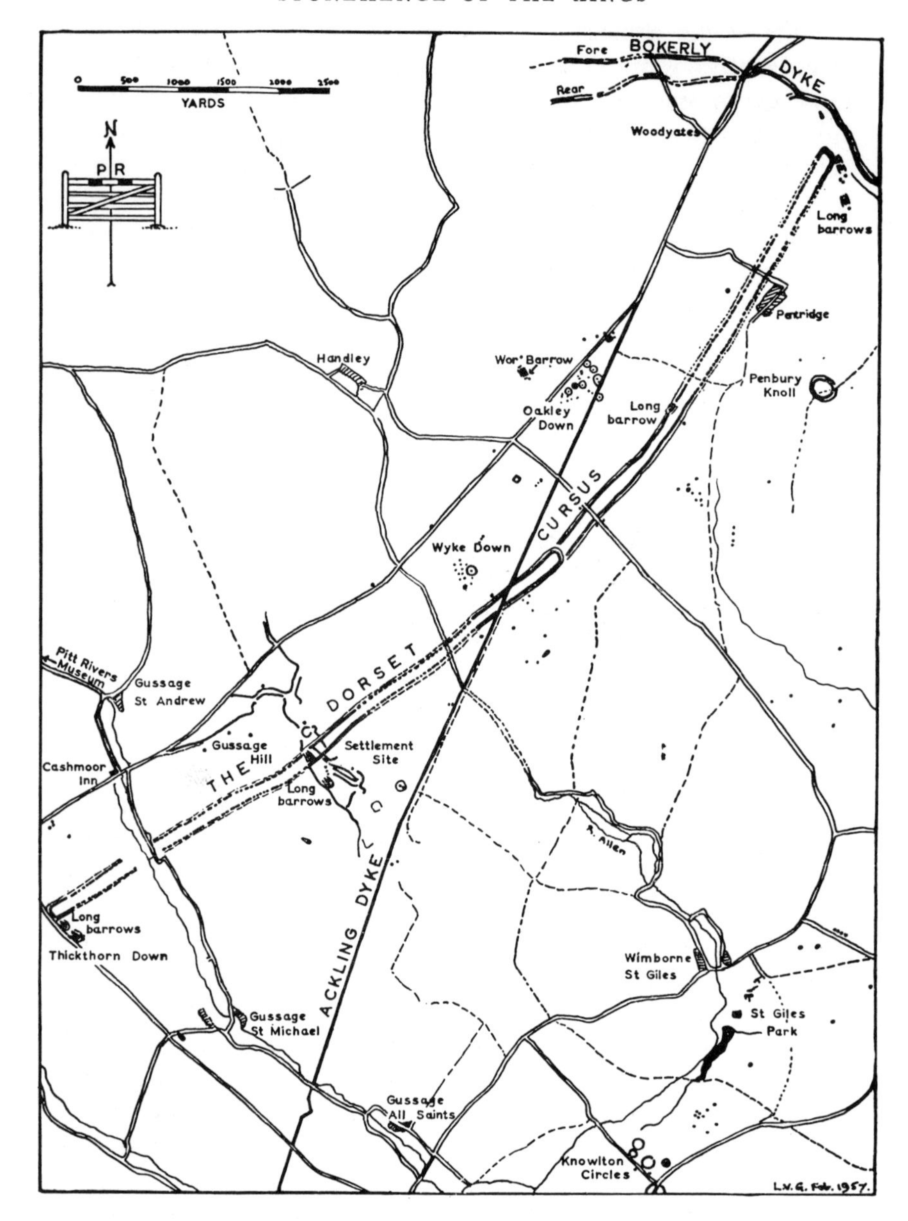

Fig. B. The Dorset Cursus, six miles long. Note the Oakley Down and Wyke Down barrow groups near it, both including Wessex Culture barrows, and also Knowlton Circles, with Wessex barrows in its region.

the life of the Bronze Age king of this province. His watchers would always be out at the port and on the coastal hills, looking for the ships of traders and raiders – the ships from the west with jadeite and tin from Brittany, tin and copper from Cornwall and gold from Ireland. Sometimes a Mediterranean ship would come with exotic beads and wine. The amber ships came from the east. At the New Year, the king would journey with his court to attend the festival at Stonehenge, bearing with him a prestige gift for the High King and votives for the gods.

If raiders came from the sea he would perform the ritual for war, his smiths would beat magic into the weapons and his priests curse the enemy; and then the King would lead out his champions and warriors, who would be exultant in the presence of their magic leader.

I thought of the introductory passage to one of the Linear B tablets found at Pylos in Greece – 'sandy Pylos', the palace of the aged hero, King Nestor, in Homer's *Iliad*. 'Thus the watchers are guarding the coastal areas.'[2] The tablet goes on to deal with military dispositions, possibly made in a vain attempt to repel the invasion of Dorian Greeks who wiped out the Mycenaean civilisation. These events in Greece would have happened a century or two after the Clandon Barrow king had died, but his world and that of Nestor's were probably not so very dissimilar. The Clandon Barrow king would have his watchers out guarding the coast, and now the great barrows on the Ridge Way above Dorchester – looking one way over the sea and the other over his kingdom – are like their memorials.

I left the first of my five 'cities' of Stonehenge Wessex and travelled north-east into the Dorset of Cranborne Chase. This is a desert of chalk like Salisbury Plain; a desert with few men, but kindly and pleasing. The road seems to glide on, straight and endless, gently up and down. At the Cashmoor Inn I turned east off the main road and stopped the car after a few hundred yards where the lane had a sharp kink in it like the starting handle of a car. The reason for this kink is that the Dorset Cursus was crossed by the lane at this point and took the lane with it, as it were, for a few yards along its eastern boundary. This cursus in Dorset outstrips even that of Stonehenge in size. It runs for the extraordinary distance of six miles and is ninety yards wide – again, pageantry and ceremonial on the grand, regal scale.

As far as I know there is no other ceremonial way comparable in scale in British history. The approaches and avenues to Windsor Castle are insignificant in comparison – the Long Walk runs south from Windsor Castle for slightly less than three miles, for instance. Great as is the Dorset Cursus, one can stand by the western seaboard of Europe at Carnac in Brittany and watch the alignment of great stones, eleven abreast sometimes, marching away into the distance, three thousand strong, worn ruins of four thousand years ago, and know that these were probably used for a similar purpose as the Dorset and Stonehenge cursuses, but at Carnac on an even more magnificent scale.

Knowlton Circles four miles east of the cursus was my objective. Further up the course of the cursus the fine group of Wessex Culture barrows on Oakley Down lies less than a mile to its west. In my opinion this great processional way, the Dorset Cursus, links the henges of Knowlton Circles and the many other Neolithic and Bronze Age monuments in the area into a single social entity; not so much a 'city' in this case – it is too scattered – but of the nature of a kingdom, with its capital at Knowlton. The Oakley Down barrow group includes six disc- and two bell-barrows, and has yielded bronze daggers, amber beads and pottery allied to Stonehenge.

I went on into a tangle of lanes leading off the eastern fringe of Cranborne Chase. Map-reading on foot is one thing; map-reading in a car when you have to concentrate on narrow bends is another. It was pouring with rain. I was lost. Away from the attraction of the coast and miles from any city, the atmosphere of this part of Dorset was that of a land unknown to any but the few people who lived there. Vague illusions hovered in the back of my mind that I could turn a corner and find an unrecorded Avebury, known only to incurious natives, confronting me. Even in the rain, it was beautiful, lost, endless – the heart of darkest, rural England.

I drove into the little village of Wimborne St Giles and went into the village shop; but even here, although I knew that Knowlton was less than two miles away the name and description of a ruined church with a great bank round it was not known. One person is drawn a long journey to see a marvel of interest; another does not know it has existed all his life a few fields away. I continued and at last saw the upper part of a square Norman tower rising above a high bank. I stopped at the entrance through the railings that protected this extraordinary site; one which is I believe unique. It has been described as the most romantic place in Britain.

I walked over the short, wet grass into the great enclosure to the church of dull red stone. Standing in the small ruined nave, I looked out through empty Gothic arches framing sections of the surrounding bank built three thousand years before the church. But here and there a rounded Norman arch showed – 1066 – the best-known date in English history. We will never know the details of such a great event as the Battle of Hastings from the England of four thousand years ago, but such events did happen. The Knowlton Circles are dead, but the people who used them were alive.

I walked over on to the top of the bank of the henge monument by some yews that had the swollen trunks of great age. In the field next to the henge a dark barrow rose twenty feet high under leafless trees. I had seen aerial photographs showing traces of other barrows around where I stood. The remnants of two other henges lie a hundred yards or so on either side of this central circle. Again the pattern of monuments of early barbarian Britain repeats itself at Knowlton. These seem as at Stonehenge the grouping of public buildings of a society ruled by a king. I think one can speculate legitimately on such a king as he who is buried in the Clandon Barrow near Dorchester travelling north towards Stonehenge at a feast and truce time like Samaine in Ireland or the Olympic Games in Classical Greece to be entertained on his journey as befitted royalty by the king at Knowlton. Fine food and drink, bards, poets, dancers, athletes, handmaidens, splendid clean clothing and baths, and the exchange of gifts would all play their part as in the royal visits in the *Odyssey*.

My mind travelled on northwards through the Wessex Culture 'cities' at Stonehenge and Avebury to Lambourn Seven Barrows in the heart of the Berkshire Downs. This last was very familiar to me. We will go to Seven Barrows later.

REFERENCES

1. Grinsell, L. V., *The Archaeology of Wessex*, Methuen, 1958.

2. Chadwick, John, *The Decipherment of Linear B*, Cambridge University Press, 1958.

CHAPTER 9

Revelation at Clickhimin

THIS BOOK began and was intended as a personal search for the people of Stonehenge. It has suddenly become a fantastic chase, with the quarry in sight – never to be caught, but visible in the distance.

I must be careful not to over-dramatise what follows now. It is as if a pyrotechnic rocket had been fired into the sky, dropping star-shells of light.

I would rate the ultimate peak in the history of archaeological achievement to be the unearthing of Mycenae by Heinrich Schliemann. The history of civilised Europe was pushed back a thousand meaningful years by one excavation. There are few achievements in the whole field of learning even comparable with this. In archaeology, perhaps Sir Arthur Evans' detailed re-creation of the even earlier and more refined Cretan civilisation, or the finding of the Rosetta Stone by the use of which Egyptian inscriptions could be translated are comparable, but the ultimate, the nonpareil, of revelation through archaeology in Europe is Schliemann's at Mycenae.

Before firing the pyrotechnic rocket, I would like to outline what Schliemann achieved at Mycenae, so that the parallel with what follows can be seen.

Schliemann was an extraordinary man. He rose from a penniless youth to great wealth by financial dealings in Europe, and through banking in the California gold-rush of 1851. By the age of thirty-three he could speak fifteen languages, one of these being ancient Greek. Consequently he could read Homer in the original; and while finance was his business, Homer was the passion of his life since childhood days.

Up to the days of Schliemann, Homer was thought of as a great poet, perhaps the greatest the world has known. But there the assessment ended. The world of Homer seemed that of fable; there was no past historical world to which the details of the society he described in the *Iliad* and *Odyssey* could be ascribed; certainly not that of Classical Greece, the documentary history of which commenced with the first Olympic Games in 776 BC. To take the most obvious discrepancy between the Homeric and Classical Greek world; the Greek forces at the Trojan War were led by Agamemnon, King of Mycenae, the undoubted leader of the many other kings and armies drawn from all over Greece, whereas the most powerful state in Classical Greece was Athens, which in the *Iliad* receives scant mention. Homer tells us in the *Iliad* that Agamemnon of Mycenae led a hundred of his ships to the attack on Troy, whereas the Athenians under Menestheus, a very minor hero in the Greek ranks, mustered only fifty. All that there was at Mycenae in Schliemann's day – and for nearly two thousand years before, as the Greek historian Pausanias testifies – were some tumbled Cyclopean walls and tombs. And yet – agreeing with Homer – many of the greatest Greek myths centred on Mycenae, not to mention Tiryns and Argos near by.

There seemed no reason why historical knowledge as opposed to seemingly mythical fantasy should ever be able to probe back before 776 BC. And then Schliemann came on the scene with his vast wealth and Homeric obsession.

He first excavated at Troy and his results astonished and in some cases antagonised scholars throughout the world. Here was an unknown civilisation which could conceivably be that of the Troy described in the *Iliad*.

He then turned his attention to Mycenae, undoubtedly the scene of his greatest triumph, and perhaps the culminating vindication of the value of archaeology as a branch of learning. Guided by the account of Pausanias and, it seemed, a sixth sense – it almost appeared that he could *smell* gold after his success in the Californian gold-rush and at Troy – he dug inside the Cyclopean wall on the featureless, rocky hillside. He uncovered the royal Shaft Graves of Mycenae – the greatest royal treasure ever unearthed in Europe.

Schliemann found five Shaft Graves, in this first discovery, in which nineteen bodies were disposed. Some of the bodies had as many as five gold diadems or crowns and as many ornate gold crosses with arms shaped like laurel leaves. In one grave alone there were eleven massive gold goblets; in another more than 700 decorated gold discs. There were gold vases and wine jars, gold belts, garters, tiaras, brooches, pins, signet-rings, bracelets, ear-rings, hairpins, miniature double-headed battle-axes, buttons, breastplates – all in gold. There was a bull's head of silver with flaring horns of gold. There were 400 round pieces of gold, which may have been coins. There were eighty bronze swords – some with golden handles, bronze daggers richly inlaid with gold and bronze cauldrons. There were vessels and adornments made of alabaster, faience, and rock-crystal, and amber and decorated plaques of ivory. The bodies of the two children in the graves were wrapped in sheet gold. Many of the adult bodies must have been almost covered with the wealth of golden adornment. The list is endless.

The artistry of much of the metalwork was superlative and highlighted the characteristic Mycenaean tradition later found over much of the Aegean and beyond. One bronze dagger, for instance, had a scene of a lion hunt inlaid on it in gold. The lion at bay before the hunters with their shields and spears makes a masterly show in the awkward tapered shape of the dagger blade.

The climax of the drama was that the male burials had gold death-masks, once moulded to their newly dead faces, and still showing something of the personality of each man when he had lived. Beneath the last of these, Schliemann looked down on an actual human face, intact with its eyes and all its flesh, which had lain there for three and a half thousand years. The obsessed Schliemann saw the face as the realisation of his mental picture of the King of Mycenae in the *Iliad.* He raised the death-mask to his lips and kissed it, and then sent a telegram to the King of Greece:

'I have gazed on the face of Agamemnon'.

In this way Schliemann revealed like a magician the truth of Homer's 'Mycenae, rich in gold'. From this success of a wayward, unacademic genius a new historical dimension was gradually born as scholars slowly realised that an immense and previously unknown Aegean civilisation was unfolding before their searches, with Mycenae as the type site. It was the first civilisation ever born in Europe, which then mothered in a sense the civilisation of the whole continent. It was not quite the world of Homer, but the *Iliad* could be partly seen in its context and the fantasies of the Greek myths were given a solid foundation to their confused, exaggerated mysticism. Greek-born archaeologists in particular have worked ever since to correlate their discoveries with Homer and the myths to achieve a truly living history of Mycenaean Greece.

The most important thing that Schliemann discovered was not the intrinsic wealth of treasure; his work extended the history of Europe by a thousand years. The study of the cultural palace and other architecture, art, pottery and such things as the seal-stones with their expressive pictures – just like those found in Crete – produced eventually an archaeological time-scale into which this great civilisation is still being fitted. In 1952 the decipherment of the Mycenaean literary texts by Michael Ventris deepened the knowledge of this forgotten civilisation.

That is Schliemann's achievement at Mycenae. He gave the archetypal fables of Europe true life. How is this relevant to Stonehenge?

Let us look at the picture we have of barbarian northern Europe. Between 2000 BC and the Roman conquest in Britain in AD 43 the picture is one of a society rapidly increasing its proficiency in metal-working; far-trading; having a culmination of a great art tradition; with a large population to build Stonehenge, Avebury, the later hill-forts and other communal buildings; and increasingly concerned with war. Professor Stuart Piggott has called this High Barbarian Europe.

The study of its archaeology has been intensive. It might be stretching it too far, but in a loose sort of way, we know the archaeology of Britain. The evolution of cultural pottery styles has been studied to the nth degree, even computers have worked on pottery shapes. Anatomists classify the races of skeletons. Pollen, which is indestructible, reveals crops grown and the natural vegetation at a site in the dated past. The correlation of pottery styles with metal goods of known affinity has been worked on with considerable success. We have dating evidence from, for instance, the faience beads of civilised countries with known datable histories, and more recently we have a form of absolute dating within limits in the radio-carbon method.

Yes, there is, and always will be, much more to find out, but in an interim sort of way, if I may put it like that, we have the archaeology. But archaeology is, or should be, a study of people, and it seems in an extraordinary sort of way that we do not have the people. As I wrote before in an earlier chapter, we know in great detail where their ceremonies took place and where their aristocratic dead were buried, but in the earlier period we scarcely know where one single person in Britain spent his everyday life. Mystic people seem to have gathered, built Stonehenge, and then vanished into nowhere like wraiths. The only possible explanation has seemed to be that these people were nomads and lived in tents or temporary homes of some kind that have left no trace. The building of their temples would then be explained by the assembly of people from a very wide area to carry out the work. In the later Iron Age we know where fighting took place, at the hill-forts, but the habitation sites are far from plentiful in spite of the fact that Pytheas, a Greek explorer, said about 320 BC that the inhabitants of Britain were very numerous. So, perhaps I may be excused again by putting it this way to develop my theme. In Britain we have the archaeology, but we do not have the people and neither do we have myths. In fact, this is Schliemann and Mycenae in reverse. He went to Mycenae knowing the myths and Homer and produced the archaeology to fit them. It would be a truly remarkable thing if one excavation in Britain could be as all-revealing as Schliemann's was at Mycenae. I wrote in an earlier chapter (before the excavation I am about to describe had been reported) that if we could find where people lived, 'it will be a great day – no! – one of the greatest days in the history of British archaeology'. I also wrote that I hoped that it might happen before I finished writing this book. I believe it has . . . I must qualify this statement by saying that this new evidence is so recent that its full implications have not yet been worked out, and I have no clear knowledge of what I will be writing by the time I am coming towards the end of this book.

What may prove to be the 'Mycenae' of northern, barbarian Europe took place on an islet known as Clickhimin in the Shetland Islands. The excavation there was directed by Mr J. R. C. Hamilton, who is Inspector of Ancient Monuments of the Ministry of Public Building and Works. The structure he was investigating was a broch. There are large numbers of these brochs on the islands and mainland of northern Scotland. They are well built forts, made of dry-stone walling; some surviving to a height of forty feet and having the general appearance of the stump of a lighthouse. Their primarily defensive nature is shown by their uncompromising walls of stone being only broken for one small lintelled entrance, which originally

built *upwards* in two and three storeys. These domestic buildings were ranged peripherally, backing against the inside of the fort rampart. Mr Hamilton describes them as 'tenemented half-timbered buildings',[2] with the first and even second floor 'flats', one might call them, reached by ladders; and the ground floor used for cattle stalls, corn-grinding, pottery-making, metalwork and so on. The rooms in the upper storey had doors opening on to the rampart walk on top of the fort. What enlightenment . . . ! No one had thought of prehistoric man living upstairs. The fort at Clickhimin had one hut in its interior, as have had so many similar forts excavated in Scotland and Ireland previously, which led to the mistaken impression that a great structure had been built for one family. Now Clickhimin and by presumption other similar forts could be seen as *clan* forts for the protection in war and weather of, it may be, a hundred in smaller forts up to great numbers for the important royal centres such as Tara and Emain Macha in Ireland. It could be seen that the barbarian clans lived in close inward-looking communities, as far as their social life was concerned, though ideally placed to rush in a moment through their living-room doors on to the rampart when the alarm was given. The Irish myths tell us that the call to arms must have been frequent from the watchers on the ramparts. After allowing for warrior vainglory, the claim of Conall Cernach the Ulster champion second only to Cu Chulainn tells the battle-lust of the age. 'I swear by that by which my people swear, since I took spear in hand I have never been a day without slaying a Connaughtman or a night without plundering by fire, and I have never slept without a Connaughtman's head beneath my knee.'[3]

The setting in which Conall Cernach makes this typical boast of a Celtic hero is brought dramatically into focus by Mr Hamilton's discovery at Clickhimin. The size of houses in Irish myth is given by one dimension – now clearly seen as the diameter of round clan forts – and the description of the house runs, for instance 'nine compartments from fire to wall'. This formerly puzzling description is now clear. One can now picture the radially-set tenements with private rooms running back towards the rampart and inward-looking balconies and windows encircling the great communal hearth. At times of drama so loved by the ancient Celts, the setting would be like that of an Elizabethan theatre, but with crowded kings and warriors looking down as from boxes on to the scene around the hearth.

At feasts, the Irish tradition was for the most famous heroes to vie with each other by boasting of battle victories or even combat at the fire where the beast was cooking for what was called the 'Champion's Portion' – the first and finest cut. There is no more dramatic myth than *The Story of the Pig of Mac Datho*. Mac Datho, the king of Leinster, had a famous hound, which was coveted by both King Conchobar of Ulster, and King Aillill and Queen Medb of Connaught. The drama is set by both parties being promised the hound and invited to come for it at the same time. The kings and champions from the two provinces attend the palace of the Leinster king and are greeted with a feast, at which a wonderful pig which has been fed for seven years on the milk of fifty cows was to be eaten. The greatest heroes come to the hearth, one by one, each seeking to hold the floor. But the Connaughtman, Cet, son of Magu, seems to win the day. He stands by the pig, knife in hand, and says, 'Find ye now one man among the men of Ireland who can contend with me, or else leave to me the dividing of the pig.'

First one Ulster hero then another challenges him, but each is shamed by some past occasion on which Cet has bested him. Cascraid the Stammerer, son of King Conchobar, is reminded of the Connaught spear thrust in the neck that produced his infirmity of speech. Cet holds the floor and prepares to cut the pig. Then Conall Cernach enters and boasts as I have written above, finishing, '. . . I have never slept without a Connaughtman's head beneath my knee'.

Cet answers, 'It is true, thou art a better warrior than I. But if it were Anluan, my brother, were here, he would match thee with victory for victory. It is bad for us that he is not in the house.' 'But he is,' declares Conall Cernach, drawing Anluan's head from his belt and hurling it on to the chest of Cet. Then Cet went from the pig, and Conall said 'Now let them come to the contest!'[4]

Let no one stand now in a Scottish broch or one of the earlier forts like Clickhimin, or an Irish stone-fort, or ring-fort where the once massive timber ramparts have rotted away – in all of which lived clans of Celtic warriors – and think the ruin dead, unpeopled. In all, they should see the packed ring of barbarian aristocrats, splendid in their gold-threaded clothes, magnificently worked adornment and weapons, clamouring down at them by the hearth, as Conall Cernach by their side says, 'Now let them come to the contest.'

Yes, because of the Clickhimin excavation, the Celtic clans are now known to have a fitting setting for their character; a strong fort, a comfortable, gregarious home, and a great theatre to play the often artificially created but deadly dramas so dear to them.

This clear vision of Celtic domestic life was not the only result of Mr Hamilton's excavation by any means. The events in the Irish myths (as in the Greek) clearly cover a wide span of time – from some dimly recorded early period to the time of the coming of Christianity in the fifth century AD. But the most concrete and explicit body of myth is the Ulster Cycle, dealing with the kingdom ruled by King Conchobar and his paramount champion, Cu Chulainn. From the mediaeval Irish antiquaries onwards there has been a general and vague agreement to date the Ulster Cycle to 'about the time of the birth of Christ'. Before the Clickhimin excavation, Professor Kenneth Hurlstone Jackson in his fine book, *The Oldest Irish Tradition: A Window on the Iron Age*, had the last and most authoritative word in 1964. He wrote that the culture described in the Ulster epic had its roots in the Gaul (for the Gauls were Celts) of the third century BC, but that the Ulster tales were put together in, say, the fourth century AD.

This statement still stands, but the Clickhimin excavation carried back the tradition of clan life in Celtic forts to the fourth to the second centuries BC. The actual events of the Ulster Cycle may not have occurred so early, but similar events would have been occurring in a similar sort of society. Why can the Clickhimin clan-fort be equated with the tales of the Ulster Cycle? I have mentioned already the now comprehensible description of a palace, 'nine compartments from fire to wall'. Other tales mention palaces with many doors with beds between the doors opening on to the rampart; a quite meaningless description before Clickhimin. Another famous tale, *The Destruction of Da Derga's Hostel*, tells of attackers lying in wait outside the walls of the hostel, and telling each other details of the various rooms and the people in them in the hostel to aid their planned assault. This had seemed the wildest flight of Celtic fancy – how could men see over a wall and describe what was going on in single-storeyed huts within? But now the numerous doors, opening on to the rampart walk, provide the quite reasonable answer.

But the conclusive evidence comes from the detailed description of a palace in the tale of *Briciu's Feast*. Briciu, of the Poison Tongue, the mischief-maker of Ulster, arranged a great feast for King

Conchobar and the warriors of Ulster, and built a new palace for the occasion. This is how it is described: 'The house had been made on the plan of Tech Midchuarta (Tara's Banqueting Hall), having nine compartments from fire to wall . . . A royal compartment had been constructed for Conchobar in the *fore-part of the palace, higher than all the compartments of the house* (my italics, P.C.). . . . The twelve compartments of the twelve chariot-warriors of Ulster had been constructed round it.'[5] At Clickhimin, Mr Hamilton found two-storeyed buildings set round inside the rampart, but facing the gate ('in the fore-part of the palace') was a three-storeyed blockhouse ('higher than all the compartments of the house'); clearly this was traditionally the home of the king, from which he could personally watch happenings in the courtyard of his palace, and in the other direction the approach outside to the most vulnerable point of defence, the gate. This seems to me to be a convincing correlation of archaeology and myth . . . the first time that this has happened to illuminate a broad aspect of human life in the British Isles of prehistory.

There are virtually no Celtic myths which centre basically in England but it seems more than probable that events similar to those described so graphically in Ireland were happening in England in the same sort of setting, for the puzzling and quite numerous farmsteads such as Little Woodbury, forty-eight feet in diameter, are now seen to be more probably massive timber-built clan-forts than Zulu-type huts.

This archaeological evidence in the British Isles can now be related to similar evidence of forts with buildings ranged against the walls on the Continent, principally in the Alpine region; so it is becoming increasingly clear that a considerable area of Celtic Europe arranged its social life in this way. Suddenly we can dimly see how many north European barbarians spent their everyday lives . . . suddenly the many years of meticulous study of pottery, pollen analysis, metal analysis, distribution maps, bones, earthworks, post-holes, proton gradiometers, are transmuted into *people*.

The evidence of Clickhimin is so revolutionary that it will take years before its full implications can be realised. I have had a number of discussions with Mr Hamilton, and he has stressed the relationship of the architectural evidence at Clickhimin to the ancient Irish annals and the writings of the classical authors about the Celts. One thing common to these written accounts is the constant attacks by

II. The ruin of Stonehenge. Note the white dots marking the Aubrey Holes just inside the encircling ditch and bank. The contemporary round barrows in the background are the Cursus Group, one of the many groups sited around Stonehenge. The processional way, known as the Cursus, runs just beyond this line of barrows.

III. The henge at Avebury, a quarter of a mile in diameter. Note that Avebury is typical of the sixty or more henges in Britain in having its encircling bank *outside* its ditch. The great truncated cone of Silbury Hill, 130 feet high, shows in the background.

IV. Looking up into the unrestored corbelled roof, nineteen feet six inches above the floor of the central chamber, under the enormous mound of New Grange. New Grange, a masterpiece of megalithic architecture and art of the third millenium, relates closely in both these skills to similar tombs in Spain.

v. One of the forty-five stones at New Grange decorated with megalithic art. Similar motifs of this highly characteristic art form occur in large numbers in the tombs of Ireland, Brittany and Spain. Here is a twin-spiral suggesting the 'eye' motif, with lozenges and chevrons.

VI. The magnificent Winterbourne Stoke Cross-roads Barrow Group, showing two bell-barrows (centre, above trees) with their level area between mound and ditch, and immediately above them, two touching disc-barrows with level platform and small mound in the centre. These two types of barrow are characteristic of the Wessex Culture.

VII. Finely worked gold breastplate from Clandon Barrow. Compare with gold breastplate from Bush Barrow (see Frontispiece).

VIII. Upton Lovell necklace, made up of amber from Denmark, shale from Kimmeridge and long, segmented faience beads from Mycenae. The Wessex Culture drew its wealth from a wide area. Miniature cup from a Winterbourne Stoke barrow.

IX. Sceptre-head of Kimmeridge shale, decorated with gold studs, from Clandon Barrow, associated with gold breastplate, bronze dagger and cup carved from amber. Assemblage resembles in specific items and magnificence that of Bush Barrow, near Stonehenge, suggesting a comparable royal burial in the Bronze Age ruins around Dorchester, Dorset.

X. How Iron Age houses have been visualized. An African-kraal-type reconstruction based on the setting of post-holes found at Little Woodbury, Wilts. Following the Clickhimin excavation, more probably this should rather be seen as a drum-shaped, vertical-walled building of more than one storey, involving complex carpentry in its construction, and housing a large unit of society.

XI. Reconstruction of the king's quarters three storeys high, overlooking the gate at Clickhimin. '. . . . the fore-part of the palace, higher than all the compartments of the house.' *(Drawing by Alan Sorrell.)*

XII. The broch at Mousa, Shetland Isles. A Celtic tribal structure, built for habitation and defence, still standing to a height of over 45 feet.

XIII. The architectural and domestic arrangements inside a Celtic fortress revealed for the first time. A reconstruction drawing showing multi-storeyed habitation at Clickhimin, Shetland Isles. People were living upstairs in fourth to second centuries BC. This, at last, makes Irish epic understandable and reflects on late prehistoric architecture and society in the British Isles.

XIV. Emain Macha—one of the significant ancient sites of the world where ruins and epic literature meet, as at Mycenae. The royal seat and stronghold of King Conchobar and Cu Chulainn. The encircling earthwork under large ring of trees has its bank *outside* ditch at this focus of war.

XV. Lambourn Seven Barrows. Bronze Age structures exclusively for the dead? A particularly fine disc-barrow shows at right-hand end of main collection, which is arranged in two rows.

XVI. 'Tara of the Kings.' Focal conjoined ring-forts, the Royal Seat and Cormac's House, demand the perpetuation of palace structures. The small domed mound, which contained faience beads, is the Mound of the Hostages, *c.* 2100 BC. The large enclosure encircling these features, Rath na Riogh, has its bank *outside* ditch – excavation has revealed an internal palisade. Confused site, right foreground, Rath of the Synods, *c.* AD 100–300

XVII. The Rillaton Gold Cup from Cornwall. A typical possession of the heroic societies of Bronze Age Europe, comparable with other gold cups at Fritzdorf and Mycenae.

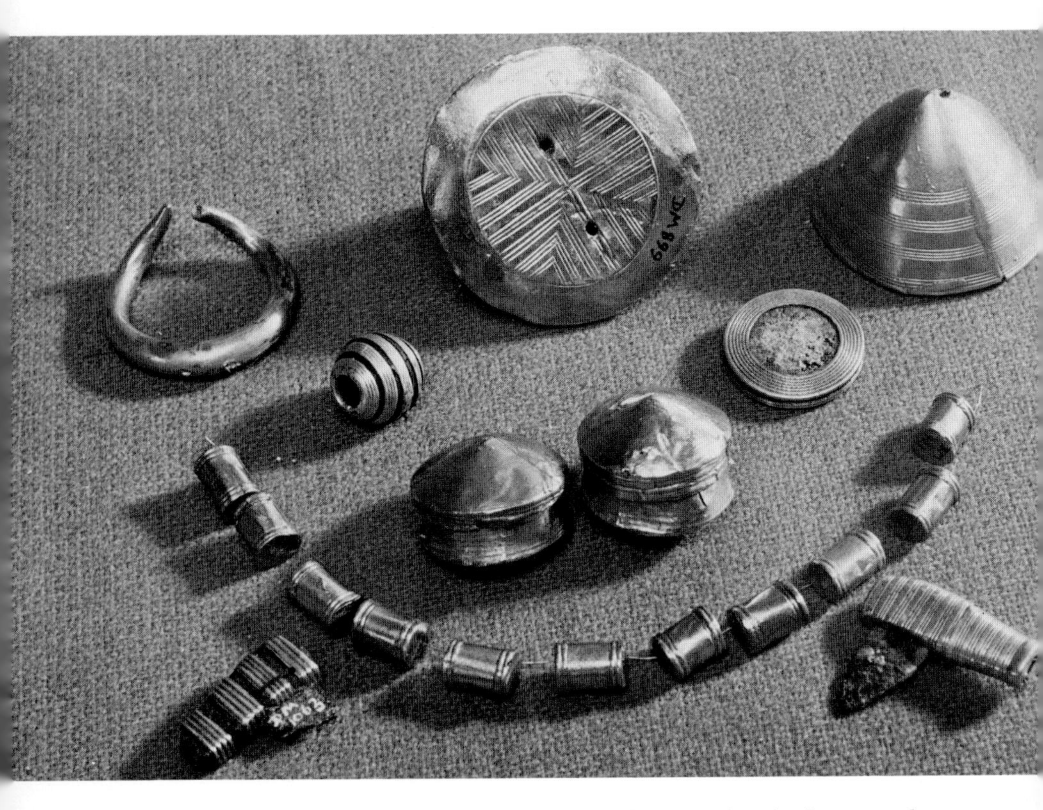

XVIII. Gold from Wessex barrows – buttons, beads, boxes and other finery. In foreground, two pendants in form of miniature halberds (a weapon common in Bronze Age Ireland and central Europe). Between two large buttons at back, gold-bound amber disc resembling those in Mycenaean world. Gold from Ireland and amber from Denmark call for an ability to voyage by sea.

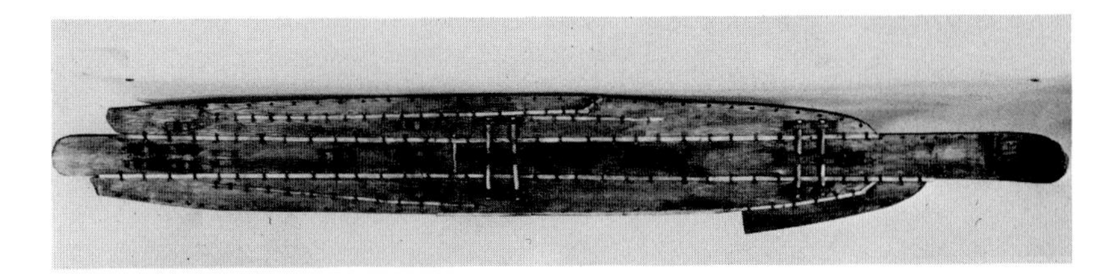

XIX. Looking down on model of remains of Bronze Age ship found at N. Ferriby, Yorks.—original over 51 feet long. Complex jointing gave rigid structure. The great length of timbers is noteworthy. Mainly bottom only survives. Bow and stern (slightly) upcurving.

XX. Adornment in Golden Barrow, Upton Lovell, Wilts. Metal objects, gold, except for small bronze knife and awl. The crescentric amber necklace, with its large plates complexly perforated for suspension, matches necklaces in Mycenaean Greece.

XXI. One of many stones in southern Scandinavia bearing Bronze Age carvings of ships. The stylised indications of design might show affinities with the Bronze Age ship found at N. Ferriby, Yorks.

XXII. Crop-marks showing prehistoric complex of structures at Stanton Harcourt, Oxfordshire. The circles are "ring-ditches," which have usually been interpreted as Late Neolithic and Bronze Age burial structures. The irregular marks are field boundaries, ways, and huts of the Iron Age. The numerous black spots are mingled pits, some with rubbish of the Late Neolithic-Bronze Age and others with rubbish of the Iron Age. A typical situation in the region, which suggests long-continued habitation through all these periods.

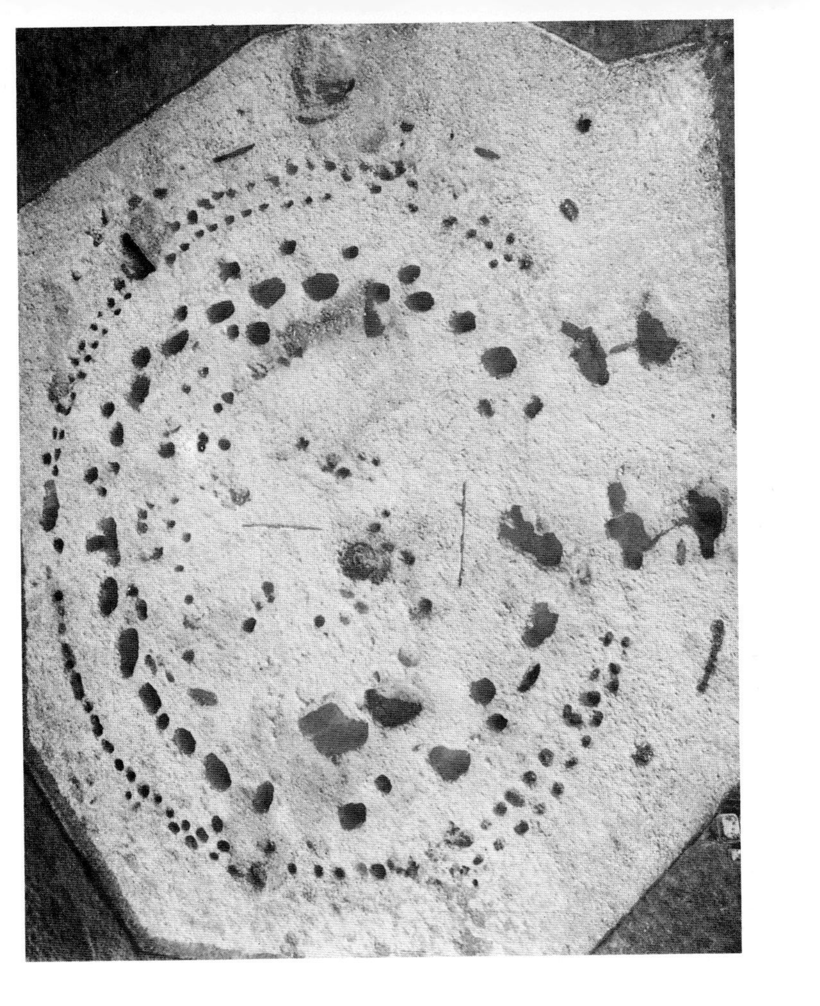

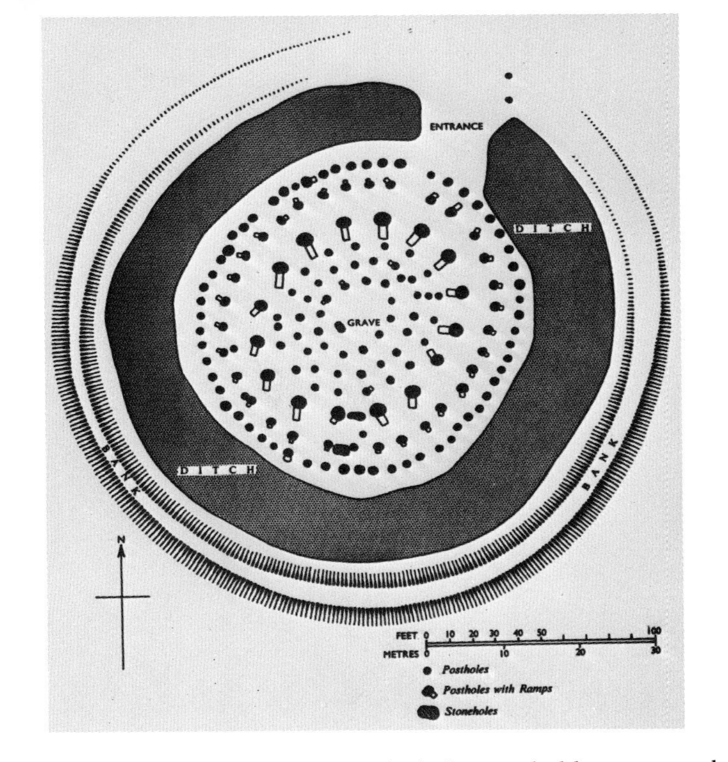

XXIII. Plan of Woodhenge (*above*) dating probably to around 2000 BC, and, (*left*) an Iron Age house at Pimperne, Dorset, currently dated to about 400 BC. (note the two rods, six feet long, for scale). The possibility of an affinity between the former, above-ground structure of the two is obvious from these ground plans.

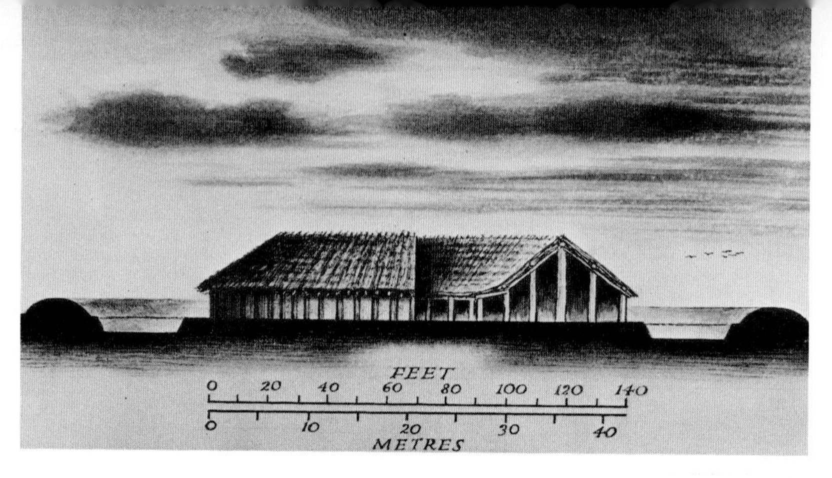

XXIV. How Woodhenge has been visualized—but a more functional design could have involved the whole roof outsloping to drain into the ditch, emphasising the ditch as a functional feature rather than a ritual one. With its massive structure, Woodhenge may well have been multi-storeyed. No undue limit should be placed on conceptions of the complexity of its design or the skill of its carpenter constructors. Clickhimin architecture and the description of palaces in Irish epic may lead towards a clear concept of this crucial building.

XXV. Finely carved stone battle-axes of the heroic societies of Early Bronze Age Britain.

xxvi. Aerial photograph of the henge at Arminghall, Norfolk. The ditches and post-hole setting (showing black) hint at structure similar to Woodhenge, with perhaps some evidence eroded.

xxvii. Aerial photograph of Woodhenge showing the rings of post-holes and ditch as dark marks. Barrow circles can also be seen that have produced evidence of stake settings and debris.

XXVIII. 'Circles' at Highworth, Wilts., resembling disc-barrows. Situated on clay and producing Romano-British pottery from ditch.

fire on forts. The great timber tenements that once existed at Clickhimin show the reason for this, and in Mr Hamilton's opinion are the explanation of the so-called 'vitrified' forts of central Scotland, where the intense heat of the burning timber has changed the stone ramparts to a glass-like substance. Many forts in Celtic Europe have what is called 'timber-lacing' in their ramparts. It was thought that this was merely a strengthening device, but here again there may be complete reinterpretation in the light of Clickhimin.

All this is in the Iron Age, say, 500 BC to AD 43. Does Clickhimin shed any light on periods earlier than this in Britain? Mr Hamilton has expressed his opinion to me that reinterpretation might well show a continuous history of circular habitation sites from the Neolithic to Iron Age times. Tentative as this is, it is an important statement. The home of Bronze Age man has never been found. Does it lie unsuspected among the many known circular structures of his period? For the moment, I finish with a question, and will turn to other aspects of Stonehenge Britain until later in the book.

REFERENCES

1. Hamilton, J. R. C., 'The Mystery of the Brochs Solved at Clickhimin', *Illustrated London News*, 11th September, 1965.

2. Hamilton, J. R. C., *op. cit.*

3. Meyer, K. (Edit. and trans.), *The Death Tales of the Ulster Heroes*, Dublin, 1906.

4. Meyer, K., *op. cit.*

5. Henderson, G. (Edit. and trans.), *Fled Bricrend*, London, 1899.

CHAPTER 10

The Irish Myths

THE IRISH myths have seldom been considered as having relevance to Stonehenge. The facts of geography must mean that they can never be directly relevant, but as time goes on I think that the indirect light they throw on Stonehenge Britain will be increasingly appreciated.

The Irish myths are the earliest description in the whole of Western Europe of the lives led by human beings. The stories are full of exaggerations, impossibilities, obscurities, discrepancies. Yet they convey a comprehensive idea of what it was like being a west European barbarian of aristocratic birth in late prehistoric times. The majority even of educated people do not know that these Irish myths exist.

The fact that we are in possession of these very early texts is to be explained by the same reason that we possess the works of Homer – the transmission from generation to generation of a learned oral tradition; in the case of Ireland, taught meticulously by the philosopher priests known as druids. This oral tradition was finally committed to writing by Christian monks from the fifth century AD onwards. The recital of the stories to the pagan Irish had beneficial and magical effects on their hearers, which in a sense could be compared to those produced by Bible readings in a Christian church. In other words, they were tales of genesis and religion.

Lebor Gabala Erenn, The Book of the Taking of Ireland, lists five invasions of Ireland before the final one.

1. Cessair (the name of the woman leader of a predominantly female invasion)
2. Partholon (the name of a male leader)
3. Nemed (the name of a male leader)
4. Fir Bolg (Fir = Men)

5. Tuatha De Danann (The Peoples of the Goddess Danann)

Little historical information can be gleaned from the specific succession of these undatable invasions; the earlier invasion stories in particular resulting from many generations of transmission produce little more than vague folk-lore. And yet I think it may just be conceivable that Cessair and her company of fifty women and three men may commemorate the tradition of the landing of the bearers of the religion of the Great Goddess. It is noteworthy that hers is the only matriarchal company.

The Tuatha De Danann were 'the most handsome and delightful company, the fairest of form, the most distinguished in their equipment and apparel, and their skill in music and playing, the most gifted in mind and temperament that ever came to Ireland. That too was the company that was bravest and inspired most horror and fear and dread, for the Tuatha De excelled all peoples of the world in their proficiency in every art.'[1]

The question arises whether Tuatha De Danann were gods. In a sense the answer is immaterial, as they were clearly reverenced in later times, and to many early peoples there was no line dividing even a living king and a god. But the name of one of their chief figures, the Dagda, is translated 'the good god' and he is described as the god of druidism and magic. The name of the goddess, Danann, may be related to that of Danu, a goddess in the battle hymns of the Indo-Europeans in India. Danu means 'stream' and may come from the same roots as the rivers Don, Dneiper, Dneister, Danube in Europe and the rivers named Don in England. The name Tuatha De Danann perhaps strengthens the Indo-European link with the southern Russian steppes, which I have referred to earlier in this book, and may carry with it a tradition of their ultimate origin.

Tuatha De Danann had four talismans: the Great Fal – the stone penis of Ireland at Tara, which shrieked under the king of Ireland; the spear of Lug against which no victory could be won; the sword of King Nuadu, which no one escaped when it was drawn from its scabbard; and the cauldron of the Dagda from which no one went away unsatisfied.

The cult of Nuadu, king of Tuatha De Danann, was probably known outside Ireland. It is thought that Nodens, a god worshipped in Roman Britain, was an equivalent deity. A temple dedicated to

Nodens at Lydney, Gloucestershire, was excavated by Sir Mortimer Wheeler. Other leading figures are Lug, the god of skills and knowledge who takes over the leadership from Nuadu, and whose name may be commemorated at Lyons, Laon, Leyden and Carlisle (Luguvalium); Dian Cecht, the 'god of health'; Manannan Mac Lir, 'god of the sea', after whom the Isle of Man is named; Mathgen, the sorcerer; Figol, the druid; Goibniu, the smith; Ogma, the mighty champion; Brigit, 'goddess whom poets worshipped'; and the Morrigan, 'Great Queen', the destructress on battlefields.

More than one authority has suggested that the cumbrous, uncouth fertility god of the Irish, the Dagda, one end of whose club can kill nine men and the other bring them to life again, is represented in his British form by the procreative be-clubbed Giant cut in the chalk at Cerne Abbas in Dorset.

The central story of Tuatha De Danann is the Second Battle of Mag Tuired. In this the Tuatha war with the most mysterious people in the Irish myths – the Fomoire. There has been much speculation on the question of their identity.

The Fomoire are represented as one-eyed beings, and sometimes as giants. Partholon, Nemed and Tuatha De Danann, as the settled people of Ireland, are all attacked in turn by the Fomoire, who are of the sea and islands and also the *Síd* mounds – the magic dwelling places, possibly including the ancient burial mounds. Alwyn and Brinley Rees say of the Fomoire, '. . . in some respects they seem to represent the feminine principle'.[2] Their ships' companies in the invasion against Partholon are predominantly female. As with the female company of Cessair, it is possible that the Fomoire represent the continuing and underlying influence of the Mother Goddess religion, which from the archaeological evidence appears to have continued to a late date in Ireland. I would not suggest that this conception need be too specific or that the Second Battle of Mag Tuired was necessarily entirely in the nature of a war of religion, but it is more than likely that the aristocratic warriors with their own gods in the settled tribes of Ireland looked down on the outlying and extra-tribal peoples with contempt and equated them in general with an outmoded, and, to them, primitive religion, to which, in fact, these less prosperous peoples would have clung longer.

There are interesting parallels between the one-eyed Fomoire and the Cyclopes, the one-eyed giants of the Greek myths. Many readers will recollect that Odysseus in his wanderings after the

Trojan War is imprisoned with twelve of his crew in the cave of a Cyclops.

Homer describes the cave '. . . we made out a cave there . . . with the entrance overhung with laurels . . . round the mouth a yard had been built with a great wall of stones . . .' And later: 'He (the Cyclops) then picked up a huge stone, with which he closed the entrance. It was a mighty slab, such as you couldn't have budged from the ground, not with a score of heavy four-wheeled waggons to help you.'

The laurel is closely associated with the Oracle of Mother Earth at Delphi. The description of the cave of the Cyclops with the forecourt of great stones and the enormous stone sealing its mouth would fit many tombs of the religion of the Great Goddess. It will be remembered that the Fomoire live partly in the world of the *Síd*, the mounds, possibly chambered tombs, of Ireland.

The Cyclops tells Odysseus, 'We Cyclopes care not a jot for Zeus with his aegis, nor for the rest of the blessed gods, since we are much stronger than they.'[3] This is certainly an expression of religious antagonism.

Odysseus expresses the same contempt for the Cyclopes as beings of an antique world as do the Tuatha De Danann for the one-eyed Fomoire. It is very surprising that the description 'one-eyed' (for which there seems no later outside explanation) still persists at the present day to describe contemptuously a state of primitive inadequacy – 'a one-eyed shack' and expressions of that nature.

A further parallel is that both Apollo and Lug appear in their respective myths as newly arriving gods of enlightenment; the four-day-old Apollo ousting Mother Earth and the unknown young warrior Lug defeating the Fomoires. I think this may all add up to the probability that the followers of the Great Goddess, and those equated with them because of their primitive way of life, were described with contempt as 'one-eyed' over much of Europe by the peoples of Indo-European ancestry who had their own triumphant gods of war.

It is interesting in view of the probable spread of the knowledge of metals round Europe in conjunction with the religion of the Great Goddess that smithing was the traditional craft of the Cyclopes (as it was that of Wayland of the Nordic myths, whose name was given to the Megalithic tomb in Berkshire); and it may also be relevant that the age-long attribution of the building of walls of huge stones – so called Cyclopean walls – such as that at the Citadel of Mycenae, may not be due just to the giant stature of the Cyclopes, but to a more specific relationship through their use of huge stones in the building of megalithic tombs for the religion of the Great Goddess.

Be this as it may, the Fomoire are ancient forces fighting against the newly arrived Tuatha De Danann, just as are the dark demons in India against the invading Aryan gods, and the Titans (born of Mother Earth) against Zeus in Greece. It seems almost inevitable that a similar tale was echoed at Stonehenge.

Tuatha De Danann are victorious in the Second Battle of Mag Tuired, thanks largely to the leadership of the new god-hero Lug, and the Fomoire are vanquished. The victors reign supreme at Tara, but finally in their turn even the Tuatha De who were 'the most gifted in mind and temperament that ever came to Ireland' had to yield to the invading Sons of Mil. The magic mound-dwellings that were the Fomoire's are then taken over by the Tuatha, the Dagda apportioning them between Lug, Ogma and himself. To himself, the Dagda allots Bruig na Boinne, 'The Mansion of the Boyne', no doubt one of the ruins now to be seen in the Bend of the Boyne centring on New Grange, which I have written about earlier.

These events of the Tuatha De Danann belong to the so called Mythological Cycle of the Irish myths – a vivid world of fantasy and magic. The Ulster Cycle, fantastic as it is, seems nearer to the world of reality, and follows the fortunes of Ulster, led by King Conchobar, at a time when it was the most warlike and strongest province in Ireland. The greatest accent is on war and the warrior, in particular the champion, Cu Chulainn.

Cu Chulainn was conceived by his mother Dechtine in typically heroic circumstances of high magic in which both the god Lug and King Conchobar, brother of Dechtine, appear to be involved. At the age of seven he took up arms on hearing Cathbad the druid say whoever did so that day would have a short life but eternal fame. Cu Chulainn demanded arms from King Conchobar and smashed up fifteen sets before being given the king's own weapons, followed by the king's chariot after smashing twelve of these. He then joined Conall Cernach, the Ulster champion, at the Look-Out Ford on Ulster's border where Conall was keeping guard. From here he raided into enemy territory and returned to Emain Macha, the royal capital of Ulster, with two wild deer tied behind his chariot, tethered swans flying above it, and displaying the heads of three champions he had slain.

Cu Chulainn and Conall Cernach eventually contend for the Champion's Portion. This leads them to go to Cu Roi mac Dairi, King of Munster, the province of death, for judgement. Cu Roi's occult power underlies the deeds of the warriors of Ireland. He is a sorcerer, 'King of the World', seldom to be found in Ireland. 'In what airt soever of the globe Cu Roi should happen to be, every night o'er the fort he chaunted a spell, till the fort revolved as swiftly as a mill-stone. The entrance was never to be found after sunset.'[4] The tradition of the round clan-fort like Clickhimin occurs here again.

Blathnat, Cu Roi's wife, tells the champions that each in turn must stand guard at night over the fort. Conall stands guard and a horrible spectre from the western sea throws him over the rampart of the fort. The next night the spectre attacks again from the sea, but Cu Chulainn swoops round it with his drawn sword in his strange warrior feat, the salmon-leap, and the spectre grants Cu Chulainn the right to the Champion's Portion. This is confirmed by Cu Roi on his return. But on arriving back at Emain Macha, Conall Cernach still disputes Cu Chulainn's superiority. One night an enormous peasant appears in Conchobar's hall carrying a block and an axe and challenges the champions that one of them may behead him on the first night, if he may behead the same warrior the second night. Conall accepts the challenge, but is unnerved after seeing the giant leave the hall carrying his own head after the beheading, and Conall does not appear the next night. Cu Chulainn in his turn beheads the peasant and the next night places his own head on the block. The noise of the axe is like 'the loud noise of a wood tempest-tossed in a night of storm', but it is brought down blunt side down and away from Cu Chulainn's head. Cu Chulainn is awarded indisputably the precedence of the warriors of Ulster. The gigantic peasant disappears. He was Cu Roi.

Cu Chulainn is then supreme and dedicated to Ulster. The dominant impulse of a warrior of a heroic society is realised. He fights with a young warrior, who has already repulsed several of Ulster's greatest champions, and is warned that it might be his returning son. 'Even though it were he indeed, I would kill him for the honour of Ulster.' Finally he carries the dead youth in his arms, and casts him before Conchobar and his court, saying, 'Here is my son for you, men of Ulster.' During the war with Connaught, the Cattle Raid of Cooley, he defends Ulster single-handed – with assistance at one stage, presumably divine, from Lug – against the Connaught army while the Ulstermen are under a spell cast by Macha the goddess. The motives of his fighting are a love of war, personal fame, and tribal feeling.

The Cattle Raid of Cooley (*Tain Bo Cuailnge*) has been described as the *Iliad* of northern Europe. The two stories have a fundamental resemblance in that both tell of heroic societies at war; of armies led by kings, with a large warrior van, both for tactical leadership and the brunt of the fighting, composed of an aristocratic class. The existence of a large mass of troops is conveyed also; they are presumably drawn from a free-commoner class.

The *Iliad* is the story of King Agamemnon leading the forces of Greece, composed of contingents from the various kingdoms under their kings or selected heroes, against the city of Troy near the Dardanelles. The fortunes of the war are portrayed as dependent on the prowess of the foremost heroes, in command, but more especially in their actual fighting quality as warriors; in out-boasting a formidable hero on the other side, and then in killing him in virtually single combat in the centre of raging battle. The slaying of one of the leading heroes means a disastrous collapse in the morale of his compatriots. The killing of Hector, the mighty panic-maker, by the great Achilles is almost a death-blow to Troy. The impending fight between these two is built to ever higher significance by the contests of lesser heroes as the *Iliad* progresses.

In *The Cattle Raid of Cooley*, Ulster is attacked by the forces mainly of Connaught (but also of other provinces – the Men of Erin) led by Queen Medb and King Aillil. The objective is the taking of the fabulous Brown Bull of Cooley; undoubtedly instancing the common practice of cattle-raiding leading to war. The army of Ulster is under a spell, so Cu Chulainn takes his stand alone on the ford between Ulster and Connaught. Here he first kills four Connaught warriors and from then on carries out guerilla warfare against the Connaught army. He also fights in single combat – with the agreement of Queen Medb – selected warriors of Connaught, usually at fords, thus delaying the rapidity of the Connaught advance. During the extremity of this period, the god Lug, Cu Chulainn's father, comes to help him. These contests culminate in the epic match with Ferdia, his friend, whom to his sorrow he finally kills.

King Conchobar and the warriors of Ulster awake at last from their spell and drive their enemies back into Connaught, the Brown Bull of Cooley and his fifteen heifers with them. Cu Chulainn stands on the bank of the River Shannon and watches the last rear-guard disappear into Connaught.

Several social factors appear in *The Cattle Raid of Cooley*. One is the profound influence that individual heroes (or champions in Ireland) can have on events in heroic societies; another, the practice of staging single combats between champions; and, still another, the importance of the territorial boundaries of kingdoms. Cu Chulainn makes his first stand on the border of Ulster, and finally drives the Connaughtmen back into their own province. The full extent of the kingdom is guarded along recognised common borders – a recurrent point in Irish myth. I will relate this last point later to Stonehenge Britain.

Cu Chulainn's life continues with the epic grandeur of war and magic of one of the Greek heroes, but the day comes when the Sons of Calatin, who have learned wizardry to conspire against him, take the field to destroy him. The omens tell Cu Chulainn that his end is foredoomed. The Morrigan has broken his chariot, and his horse, the Grey of Macha, resists being harnessed to it, weeping tears of blood. On his way to combat he passes two beautiful maidens lamenting as they wash a blood-stained garment at a ford. He continues and three hags, who have cooked a dog, offer him a joint from it. A geis (taboo – a common feature in Irish myth) compels him to refuse it as he would be eating his namesake (Cu Chulainn means the Hound of Culann); another geis compels him to partake of the fare at any cooking-hearth he passes. He eats and his geis is broken – a sign of impending death.

Cu Chulainn attacks alone the force of the Sons of Calatin. Pairs of contending warriors have been placed by the enemy and Cu Chulainn is provoked into intervening between them, thus placing himself in the magically vulnerable position between alternatives described in Chapter 3. After great slaughter, at last Cu Chulainn is wounded by an enemy cast of his own spear, and his bowels come forth. The enemy consent to his gathering them to him and going to a lake where he washes and drinks. An otter comes to drink the blood and he kills it with a stone – killing his namesake, the 'water-dog'. Knowing he is dying, Cu Chulainn ties himself to a pillar-stone, to die still standing. He remains thus with the hero's light over his head and the wounded Grey of Macha defending him. At last birds descend on his shoulders and he is dead. An enemy ventures forward to arrange his hair and to cut off his head. The warrior is Lugaid, son of Cu Roi. Cu Chulainn's sword falls from his dead hand and cuts off Lugaid's right hand. Cu Chulainn's right hand is cut off in return and is buried with his head at Tara.

Thus very briefly summarised ends one of the greatest epic lives outside those of classical origin. Barbarous, savage, cruel – and yet Cu Chulainn is not always merciless, and claims he does not kill women. Perhaps 'savage' is not right; the ethics of barbarism are revealed.

The society portrayed in the Ulster Cycle is similar to the heroic societies revealed in Homer. King Conchobar is the directive power controlling the life of his people; and his champion, Cu Chulainn, although a force to himself in some ways, is yet the instrument for imposing Conchobar's wishes. Cu Chulainn's status and office appears similar to that implied in the Mycenaean Linear B tablets which write of a 'Leader of the Host'. Etymologists think this office corresponds to Commander-in-Chief. The tablets say that the Leader of the Host had a household independent from that of the king, and this is implied in the Ulster tales of Cu Chulainn. A status next to the king appears in both cases. Cu Chulainn is an instrument of the king through whose symbol he expresses his own great prowess. Conchobar's kingdom was designed for the purpose of war, and in war Cu Chulainn expressed almost his entire nature.

Many of the royal capitals of Ireland have myths of the death and burial of female foundresses at them – Carmun at Carmun, Naas at Naas, Macha at Emain Macha and so on. These clearly take the nature of goddesses and are fertility deities presiding over their separate lands. In some myths the nature goddess is actually named Sovereignty to whom the king must be wedded to take over his realm. Some authorities equate these goddesses, such as Macha, with the Great Goddess religions of the Mediterranean, and I think that here once again we have the possibility of a conception revealed in the Irish myths supporting the evidence shown at Stonehenge with its Mother Goddess carving. The earliest monument at Tara is a passage grave of the Goddess religion, and perhaps the roots of a goddess stem tenuously back to this tomb, giving an immemorial sanctity to the later Indo-European royal palace.

After Mr Hamilton's excavation at Clickhimin, the society in which Cu Chulainn lives is illuminated brilliantly. In such a congested, inward-looking clan-fort, internal dissension was inevitable; yet, just as inevitable would be the fierce antagonism to tribes outside the walls of the fort as a quarrelsome family closes its ranks to outside danger. The tribal fort was a cell, a small world of its own. The traditional significance to Irishmen up to the present day of the peat fire that never goes out is now clearly identifiable with the great hearth central in the palace 'with nine rooms from fire to wall'. It was the focus of his small world, his vital food in the great cauldron, his vital warmth, his drama of 'the Champion's Portion' – the Irishman's life almost literally revolved around his tribal fire. It is interesting that a constant feature of the Mycenaean palace is the great hearth in the King's throne room. I think it is possible that this tradition was held by the people of Stonehenge, and I will come back to this later.

The subtle Celtic mind projected the little world of the tribal fort with its central hearth into the larger world of Ireland as a whole. Uisnech in Westmeath where the Great Assembly at the festival of Beltaine took place, was said to be the centre, the navel, of Ireland, and it was here that Mide the druid lit the first fire from which every chief hearth in Ireland was kindled. This conception of the centre was present also at Delphi, where the Pythoness sat on the Omphalos, the navel, the centre of the world, to make her prophecies. As Apollo took over the Delphic Oracle, so the tongues of the earlier druids at Uisnech were cut out and buried under its ground by Mide, who then sat upon them.

After the Clickhimin excavation, the tales of another cycle of Irish myths, the Fenian Cycle, can be seen in a clearer light. While the Ulster Cycle is concerned with the fortunes of a province nucleated in an introverted society inside the walls of Emain Macha, the Fenian Cycle deals with Finn mac Cumaill, leader of a body of highly trained warriors, living and roving in the hills and woods of Ireland. The very distinctive nature of this life to Irish eyes can now be seen by its contrast to the crowded, static life of most Irishmen living around the tribal hearth.

That such bands of warriors were an acknowledged and respected institution in Ireland is clear from the texts of the myths. They had the duties of policing the country, and the protection of Ireland as a whole against invasion from outside.

The setting of the Fenian tales in the 'greenwood' of Ireland, as it were, gives them a romantic, Arcadian quality. A poem of typically Celtic beauty comes from the tale of Diarmaid and Grainne.

> 'Arran of the many stags, the sea reaches to its shoulder; island where companies were fed, ridges where blue spears are reddened. . . . It is delightful when the fair weather comes, trout under the brinks of its streams, seagulls answer each other round its white cliff; delightful at all times is Arran.'[5]

There is a nostalgia in the tales of the Fenian Cycle which made an understandable appeal to the Romantic Movement in the last century. They transport one deep into the Celtic twilight.

A close parallel exists between the story of Diarmaid and Grainne, and that of Aphrodite and Adonis. Both Grainne and Aphrodite are the wives of war-leaders, Finn and Ares, the god of war, respectively. They both take the active, dominant part in inducing Diarmaid in the one case, and Adonis, in the other, to love them. Both Diarmaid and Adonis are finally slain by boars. It is possible that these two tales both contain a memory of the annual sacrifice of the young fertility god during the time of the power of the Great Goddess.

The tale of the woman Blathnat, 'Little Flower', seems similarly to have a parallel in the Mediterranean. Cu Roi, 'the man in the grey mantle', King of Munster, province of death, comes three times at the year's end demanding Blathnat from Cu Chulainn. Cu Roi then takes Blathnat to Munster, but Cu Chulainn wins her back again at the year's end. Blathnat seems a similar figure to Persephone in Greece, who is carried down to the underworld by Hades, and only reappears each year at the spring, bringing its new growth with her.

Ireland is Ireland, and Stonehenge is in England. But as I wrote at the beginning of the chapter, I think the Irish myths will increasingly be looked on as relevant to the world of Stonehenge as parallels giving some indications of what Stonehenge's world was like. I think that in these tales many of the gods and goddesses and the deeds of warriors are set out in some sort of equivalent Irish form to those of Stonehenge. Stonehenge was built before the time at which the main events in the Irish myths took place, but that Tara was a great centre well before the apparent date of the Irish myths is shown by the passage grave there, the Mound of Hostages, which was in use around 2100 BC as we have seen. A secondary burial was found in the Mound of Hostages interred with faience beads, those significant trading beads from the eastern Mediterranean. This argues the importance of Tara in the Stonehenge period, as faience is a rare find in the British Isles away from the trading lure of Stonehenge itself. I think that many threads from a long period of regard for the great people and events associated with such royal sites in Ireland were drawn into the myths we have before us now. The Christian monks who finally wrote down the oral traditions of Ireland have tended to obscure, because of religious antagonism, the pagan divinity of many of the figures in them, but there is much evidence that these figures were indisputably divine – that in fact here in often disguised form are the prehistoric gods and goddesses of Ireland.

Mr T. G. E. Powell of Liverpool University has written in his book, *The Celts*:

> 'The Celts in Ireland preserved a western peripheral fastness of Indo-European tradition as, at the oriental end of the range, did the Aryans of Northern India. These long survived the disappearance of their geographically intermediate common parentage.'[6]

The myths of Greece lay in the spread from this 'geographically intermediate common parentage', and I think, in their own particular but related form, so did the lost myths of Stonehenge. The myths of Ireland and Greece have many similarities, and I think, did we but know them, the myths of Stonehenge would be equally akin. Allowing for the later date of many of the Irish myths, I think a comprehension of the Irish myths is as near as one can get to an understanding of the people of Stonehenge Britain. In time it may appear that this is nearer than is generally thought at present.

The essence of the Irish myths is the constant portrayal of heroic tribal societies; societies whose economy was based not on commercial trade but on war and loot from neighbouring tribes, activated by the king and warrior aristocracy. Fundamental to comparative wealth, power, and the prestige of hospitality was the possession of livestock in increased numbers, and, apart from an innate lust for war, the acquirement of this and other loot was one of the main themes in heroic life, exemplified in Ireland by *The Cattle Raid of Cooley*. It is in this way that I see also the social impulses of human life in Stonehenge Britain.

REFERENCES

1. Fraser, J. (Trans.), *Ériu, VIII.*

2. Rees, Alwyn and Rees, Brinley, *Celtic Heritage*, Thames and Hudson, 1961.

3. Homer (Trans. E. V. Rieu), *The Odyssey*, Penguin, 1946.

4. Henderson, G. (Edit. and trans.), *Fled Bricrend,* London, 1899.

5. Rees, Alwyn and Rees, Brinley, *op. cit.*

6. Powell, T. G. E., *The Celts*, Thames and Hudson, 1958.

CHAPTER II

Tara of the Kings

TARA, WITH some of the other royal sites in Ireland, is unique in northern Europe in that the ruins that can still be seen there relate in various ways to an extensive corpus of mythological, epic, and proto-historic documentary material. The importance of Tara from at least 2000 BC up to the third century AD has been revealed by archaeology. The myths, with Tara already an important centre, commence at an early period which it is impossible with what is known at present to specify, although the texts suggest a period deep into the equivalent pre-documentary times in Britain. Irish culture was never disrupted by Roman conquest, and the Iron Age there – which ended in Britain in AD 43 – continued to the fifth century AD, when the arrival of Christianity caused cultural changes. Tara as a royal seat was abandoned, according to the proto-historic accounts, in the sixth century AD due to clashes between the Irish Christian saints and the king of that time, Diarmaid.

The persistence of the early Irish stories was first due to the Celtic tradition of oral learning and the diligent teaching of tribal lore by learned men of the druidic class. This carried the lore through the later days of prehistory. Tradition says that in the third century AD Cormac mac Airt, High King of Tara, commanded his chroniclers to write the tales down, and St Patrick had their chronicling continued in the fifth century AD. Druidic and bardic colleges flourished alongside the monasteries, leading to a priceless body of manuscript literature, such as the *Book of Leinster* dating from the twelfth century but drawn from the far earlier oral lore, which itself depicted events earlier still, being available to us. Just as Homer shows us life in words at a very early period in the Mediterranean, so the Irish annals do the same for a part of north-western Europe. Much of this material focuses on Tara.

This Irish saga and epic material is scarcely known – except to a few scholars – outside Ireland, and is little known to the general public of Ireland itself. Surprisingly, it has never been published in an English translation from the Irish in popular form, the only works available being rare books published fifty years or so ago. Ireland is now predominantly English-speaking, and that its people should be cut off from their marvellous archetypal tales – *The Cattle Raid of Cooley* has been described as the *Iliad* of northern Europe with a considerable degree of aptness – is astonishing. British and other English-speaking archaeologists have had little opportunity to assess Irish mythological material against their own studies and it may be that when this is fully undertaken – coupled with the recently acquired knowledge at Clickhimin – a flood of understanding will come rushing in from all sides. A golden age of great archaeological advance could be the result. Some fine work has been done in Ireland itself, but a more general awareness of this almost untapped literary material relating to the distant past could be one of the most exciting elements in the study of prehistory today. The type of society that existed at least back to the third century BC is shown vividly. A tool lies to the hand which has scarcely been used. How different from the great flowering of translations of the *Iliad* and *Odyssey* and the profuse literature, both for scholars and people in general, commenting on them.

So, just across the Irish Sea, there are monuments and literary material which can be related to prehistoric times in Britain itself. On the archaeological side, what do you see at Tara? The earliest monument is the Mound of the Hostages, a passage grave in the tradition of megalithic architecture, dated by the radio-carbon method to about 2100 BC. It shows on its stonework the far-travelled motifs of megalithic art, including concentric circles and a 'snake' design. Forty secondary burials, dating from the Middle Bronze Age, were found in the nine-foot mound, one of them being the inhumation of a youth with a necklace of amber, bronze, jet and faience, recalling the grave-goods in the Stonehenge capital.

The Mound of the Hostages is set inside the oval earthwork known as Rath na Riogh, the Royal Enclosure, which is over 300 yards long. It has an outer bank and its internal ditch was eleven feet deep. The finding on excavation of evidence of a great wooden palisade just inside this was described by the late Professor S. P. Ó Ríordáin as 'unexpected'. This would not be so in view of recent evidence, leading us away from a mystic world of ritual to that of war.

Inside Rath na Riogh are two conjoined ring-forts. A phallic stone, reputedly the Stone of Fal, now stands in one of them. Clustered about outside are five more ring-forts, two of them being on the steeply falling brow of the hill giving the central enclosed mounds an air of commanding military defence. One of these has a small barrow-like mound in its centre, and a neighbouring ring-fort, Rath Grainne, has a circle faintly defined in its centre, perhaps suggestive of circular structure.

In some ways the most interesting structure at Tara is called the Banquet Hall. This is a sunken strip about eleven paces wide and 750 feet long, lying between two parallel banks, and running up the hill-slope toward the main group of monuments. The name Banquet Hall is applied from the writings known as the *Dinnshenchas*, ascribed to the tenth century AD.

A strange conflict arises here. Many writers of the present day believe that this long structure is in fact the ruin of Tara's Banquet Hall. In a land where nearly all early structures are circular, what an extraordinary building this would have been – narrow, but 250 yards long, and its length on a considerable slope. However, the early chroniclers named it as such and this was accepted in the last century by the Ordnance Survey in Ireland.

It must be remembered that the Banquet Hall's naming in the *Dinnshenchas* took place four centuries after Tara ceased to be a seat of kingship; indeed, it seems quite probable that Tara on its exposed hilltop was deserted by that time. In my opinion, it seems certain that the name Banquet Hall must have been misapplied to this structure in the *Dinnshenchas* from one of the circular ring-forts at Tara. In one of the most famous of the Irish tales, *Briciu's Feast*, Tara's Banquet Hall is described as being 'nine compartments from fire to wall', clearly after Clickhimin the description of a circular building. The twelve compartments of the twelve chariot-warriors are described in the annals as constructed around that of the king, again suggesting a round building, as does the Banquet Hall's other name, 'The House of the Mead Circling'.

In conversation with Professor M. J. O'Kelly, one of the leading Irish archaeologists (to whom I am grateful for advice), I was much interested and encouraged by his agreement with me that the Banquet Hall looked more like a ceremonial way in its design than a building, and Professor R. J. C. Atkinson has met me with similar agreement. To use the word 'cursus' would be unjustifiable as in

Britain structures so named are dated to Late Neolithic times, and there is no archaeological dating evidence from the Banquet Hall. However, I think the Banquet Hall, mounting the hill towards the main Tara ruins, is a ceremonial way, and general in type as such ways can be, its resemblance to the Great Cursus at Stonehenge is suggestive of one of the features common to the centres of Late Neolithic and Bronze Age ruins in Britain. If this should be so, the account of the inauguration of Conaire as King of Tara may illuminate ceremonies at Stonehenge. Advised by a bird-man the boy, Conaire, approached Tara naked. Three kings awaited him on each of the four roads to Tara, and dressed him in royal clothes. He mounted a chariot and was installed as High King. Is the so-called Banquet Hall the only survivor of the four roads to Tara? Is it a cursus? Future excavation may tell us.

The large enclosure at Tara, Rath na Riogh, has points of resemblance to Durrington Walls in the Stonehenge complex, both in the large area it encloses and in the fact that it has an outer encircling bank with an inner ditch. Superficially, there are a number of similar features between Woodhenge and the ring-forts at Tara. The association of these roughly circular earthworks with great enclosures at the two centres may not be without significance.

In Tara we have a known royal centre. Its ruined buildings still exist. With the ruins we have great tales of individual kings and the deeds of their peoples. One turns to close neighbouring Britain to seek Tara's counterpart. It is difficult to find it other than in the Stonehenge complex of monuments.

Without any wish to affront, I think that Irish archaeology (backed if not prompted from outside sources) is inclined to be set on a course that makes the interpretations of many of its ring-forts as unrealistic as possible. Surely G. Bersu, the German archaeologist, stated the truth about many ring-forts in 1945 – that the whole area inside the encircling earthwork was a large roofed building. This is the view held by Mr J. R. C. Hamilton at the present time. The frequent, but in my opinion misinterpreted, evidence of 'enlargements' or 'subsidiary lean-to buildings against the rampart' must surely point to the large, clan households described in the sagas, corresponding archaeologically to concentric circles of post-holes left by a big timber building. Irish archaeologists interpret this type of evidence as that of a hut surrounded by a palisade.

Misinterpretation of the strongholds of clans as the simple homes of a farming family has led to the most recent statements of the typical form of Celtic society being one scattered in very small units. Little now substantiates this. The Irish epics constantly describe great concourses in palaces with kings, warriors, womenfolk and attendants present in all their numbers. The kings and warriors sat in their raised 'imdai', like theatre boxes, looking down into the central hall. Unlimited feasting is dwelt upon. It is evident that all these people then slept in the rooms of these palaces, sometimes 'nine compartments from fire to wall', and did not go stumbling off into the night to innumerable small huts (the interpretations properly allow of no other term), the evidence of which does not exist. The fighting resulting from the contests of the Champion's Portion could not have taken place ringed by crowds of people in the structures so far visualised as major habitations by Irish archaeologists.

Ancient Irish tales always tell an exaggerated story – everything is larger than life. But it would be unwarranted to believe that their social life was something fundamentally different from this – that in fact these great meetings and feastings in buildings of kings and their followers did not take place at all. Classical writers describe exactly the same royal feasts amongst the Celts of Gaul. It is certain that the Irish feasts could not have taken place in the huts so far suggested in nearly all cases by archaeology. The descriptions are too circumstantial and oft-repeated to brook disbelief in their essential social significance. The whole tenor of Irish epic points to close-knit societies surrounding their kings, and certainly not to non-gregarious family groups living in scattered isolation, as its basis.

The title of this book has been chosen to parallel Tara of the Kings. Excavation at Tara has not yet been very extensive. That of the Mound of the Hostages and Rath na Riogh has been mentioned. The ring-fort, Rath of the Synods, was excavated and produced dating evidence of 1st–3rd centuries AD. Five centrally placed burials were also found in this ring-fort, and this will be referred to again later. The dating evidence available at Tara therefore is 2100 BC (the Mound of the Hostages), the Middle Bronze Age burials, and 1st–3rd centuries AD. Small finds have included the magnificent Tara Torcs of gold by the Rath of the Synods from the later part of the Bronze Age.

Dating evidence is prolific in the Stonehenge capital generally, and perhaps this from Tara is not extensive, but taking into account the early dating of many ring-forts elsewhere in Ireland and that the datings at Tara do span the period of the monuments at Stonehenge, I consider that there is good reason to view Britain's world of Stonehenge as having kinship with that of Tara. This kinship is strongly reinforced by the presence at Tara of Mediterranean faience, which brings it into the busy world of extensive European trade so evident at Stonehenge. It suggests again the power of great personages in Tara's Bronze Age able to attract wealth to themselves, as did the Wessex Culture.

As you stand at Tara, the 'high place' of Ireland, looking over the royal pastures of the plain of Meath, I think there is good reason for the mind to link the scene with the great grazing plateau surrounding the ruins of Britain's greatest prehistoric capital.

Looking back now after Clickhimin, it appears bizarre, a strange predilection in modern thought, that the earthworks at Tara were most frequently ascribed to ritual purposes. Now, the structural evidence at Tara, and the epic and proto-historic accounts all make a comprehensible whole, with provision made for palace households, a large static population, and its defence through periods of much warfare. Tara shows evidence of some kinship with the Stonehenge capital. Perhaps, before long, we will look back and think how equally bizarre was the exclusive ascription of all the monuments of the Stonehenge capital to purposes of religion and the ritual of the dead. Where were the living if not in these Stonehenge ruins?

CHAPTER 12

The Fifth 'City' and the Road to Stonehenge

I CAN look up through my window as I write to the line of Streatley Hill. This is the abrupt end, dropping to the Thames, of a chalk ridge running for fifty miles to the plateau of Salisbury Plain. Because of lack of water, this ridge of the Berkshire and Wiltshire Downs is uninhabited. It has no road crossing it from east to west and few from north to south; communication across it is by track. Away from the infrequent roads, it is little known to man. Dartmoor, measuring about forty miles square, has been called the last waste left in southern England, but the downland waste of Wessex is far bigger and little better known.

For ten years I have explored this chalk desert, seldom seeing other human beings. The absence of man is its special quality, as, say, it is that of the Libyan Desert; there is complete, uncluttered freedom, just earth and domed sky, with the smooth slopes of green-covered chalk running ten miles into the distance. Paradoxically its very austerity associates it in my mind with the warmth of great music, poetry and painting, and gives it the unity of works of human genius.

It must be true to say that the antiquities of the Berkshire Downs still hold innumerable secrets that could shed light on Stonehenge man. Some excavation has been done there over the last century, but scarcely enough to do more than touch the fringe of potential knowledge. Outside the very heart of Wessex, the remains show that it was one of the most favoured habitational areas of Stonehenge man.

I was first attracted to the study of the Berkshire and Marlborough Downs by the unique green road which runs for forty miles on them called the Ridge Way. The dense antiquities bordering the line of this natural, watershed route, now confined between hedges in a modern rural landscape, show that this was a line of travel and settlement of Stonehenge man.

In 1958, I studied its length from Avebury to the Thames crossing at Streatley by making a three-day expedition on foot with my archaeological and camping equipment and supplies carried on a pack-donkey as the most suitable load-carrier on an unmade, grass and chalk track. The intellectual research of this expedition was greatly supplemented for me by its physical novelty and pleasure. As that great archaeologist, Sir Richard Colt Hoare, said of his similar journey along the Ridge Way on horseback a century and a half ago, 'To every lover of antiquity, or of fine prospects, I strongly recommend this delightful ride.'[1]

My wife and I set out from Avebury on a beautiful June day that is a pleasant memory. On that day, there was an unmodern peace as we walked unhurriedly, over eight hundred feet up, noting and photographing the antiquities, topography and changes in the track, with the donkey, Jenny, causing small crises by trying to roll occasionally to try and rid herself of her load.

For all the peace of the journey, it was stimulating to be walking on part of a recognisable route of Stonehenge man. The remains of his communities are by it and by its continuation, the Icknield Way, going into Norfolk.

That evening we halted at Foxhill, thirteen miles from Avebury. My wife returned home and I was joined by a lifelong friend, Dr Basil Phillips. The hardship of primitive travel was made plain to us by a night of torrential rain spent in a leaking tent pitched on the track at Foxhill.

The next day in lashing rain we literally squelched on to White Horse Hill, the inscrutable subdued air of the donkey unchanging in fine and rain, as it has been in thousands of years of servitude to man. From there we were warmed and dried in contrasting brilliant afternoon sunlight until we pitched our tent again on the Ridge Way near Scutchamer Knob, the biggest barrow on the Berkshire Downs; and it was like the Islands of the Blessed where apples ripen twice a year and heroes are happy and know no death.

So to the Thames at Streatley on the following day, our experience having been that of a Stonehenge man on the same journey – the warmth of sun after cloud, dryness after rain, the pleasure of sight, tiredness, food, sleep; Pandora's Box most releases hope to man from the elements of his environment. Recorded in my mind and on film were many miles of terrain used by Stonehenge and Celtic man. The area which was most peopled in late prehistory was that neighbouring on White Horse Hill. Here there are the chambered tomb known as Wayland's Smithy, Lambourn Seven Barrows, the Idlebush group of barrows, Uffington Castle, Alfred's Castle, Hardwell Camp, the Bronze and Iron Age enclosures on Rams Hill, a prehistoric system of fields two thousand acres in extent, and the White Horse itself.

The White Horse is an extraordinary, perhaps repellent, figure, with the suggestive power of an attenuated limbed bronze of Henry Moore. The stylised art form of the White Horse, strange to our eyes, is preserved in the metal work of the incomparable Celtic tradition known as La Tène. Sisyphus-like, it is doomed to gallop wildly up the hill for ever. It takes with it Celtic love of excess and war; and the spirit of the Morrigan of Ireland, spreading fear and carnage on the battlefield, can be seen in it as it careers upward. Another goddess in Ireland, Macha, died racing against the horses of King Conchobar and the association of Celtic goddesses with horses, more strictly mares, is very strong. Epona, the most widely worshipped Celtic deity in Europe, is associated with horses in the statuary of her cult. She guided the souls of the dead to the Otherworld. It is possible that the White Horse presided over a cult centre of religion and chieftainship, with something of a parallel to that of Nodens, derived from King Nuadu of Tuatha Dè Danann, at Lydney in Gloucestershire, and with faint echoes of Tara itself.

Standing at the end of the Manger, the dramatic sculptured combe beneath the White Horse, the scene looking up in winter, with the sere yellow grass hanging down the enclosing walls, and the abrupt, flat-topped knoll of Dragon Hill rising like a golden keep on the left, displays the variations of a visual symphony in gold.

The most significant evidence of Stonehenge man in the area is Lambourn Seven Barrows. Here the barrows lie like a village street in two parallel rows at the side of the former course of a stream, with many outlying barrows scattering away. There are three disc-barrows and at least two bell-barrows in the collection, which numbers about forty (the identification of a few features as barrows is open to question).

Many of the main ruins of the Late Neolithic and Bronze Age are grouped by rivers: Stonehenge, Avebury, Dorchester – and Seven Barrows is similarly placed. The everyday needs of water probably caused this selection of site, as well as the magic attributed to the fertile source of water, as with the Celtic goddess of the River Boyne, Boand, in Ireland.

How extraordinary are these great concourses of the dead! Where are the ruins left by the once living? Surely here amongst these barrow structures, circular, but otherwise in their form of diverse shape must lie the answer. With a void elsewhere, attention must be concentrated on these simple-seeming but in fact puzzling and complex structures to find the homes of comfort-loving barbarians. Bronze Age homes have been sought over great areas and not found. Surely they must lie somewhere in the only ruins that do exist, so significantly often by rivers and near the head-waters of streams, as at Lambourn.

Traditional thought, even learned thought, is slow to emerge from its entrenchments. For centuries scholarship has been amazed by the apparently untoward ability shown in the building of Stonehenge by man so long ago. In Victorian times this amazement added to the emotional pleasure of looking back. Let us now accept Stonehenge and its contemporary more perishable buildings on their own terms and from this acceptance appreciate that Stonehenge society was complex, socially graded, rich, and outstandingly able to cope with its environment; far nearer to the historic barbarians that we know such as King Cunobeline than to wanderers, lost and subdued in their environment; with kings commanding armies of warriors, with men of specialised intellectual powers, and with great resources of human labour; royal kingdoms quite unlike anything before in Britain. Surely this is what the archaeology has told us now, and that they did not live in the open air.

The recent excavation of a bell-barrow on Farncombe Down, three miles south-west of Lambourn Seven Barrows, revealed a complex structure that need not necessarily be sepulchral; in fact, no burial was found in it. In the central area, an approximately circular setting of stake-holes, about a hundred in number and thirty feet in diameter, was found. The interpretation was that a wattling revetment had held a drum-shaped turf-stack, piled with grass down, about four feet high. Just outside the turf-stack a large piece of charred timber was found and there were a number of burnt areas of soil. There was unweathered pottery, flint, animal bone and blackened soil in the structure. The range of date of the pottery was a thousand years from the Neolithic into the Bronze Age. This type of evidence is not uncommon from some recent excavations with modern techniques. It is puzzling, but this is clear; the domed turf over barrows does not always cover a simple heap of earth; nor does it always cover a burial.

Lambourn Seven Barrows is one of the many places to reveal evidence of the style clothing took in Stonehenge time. One of the barrows contained a bronze dagger still showing the impression of the weave of woollen material in which it had been wrapped, and it can be assumed that woollen garments were worn. Evidence of the seeds of flax have been found at this time, and so clothing may have been made of linen, although flax may have been grown solely for its nutritious linseed-oil.

One barrow at Seven Barrows contained large, well-made shale buttons, as have a number of others elsewhere. The association of buttons seems earlier in the Stonehenge phase; later, long bronze and bone dress-pins were fashionable. The inference is that buttoned leather jackets were worn earlier and that the long pins were highly suitable for fastening a woollen cloak. No doubt, the workmanship of clothing for the aristocracy was of a high order, and it was probably dyed in gay colours, perhaps using some of the decorative motifs used in their pottery. Finely made-up furs would draw envious glances as do mink coats today. The recurrent finding of bronze razors also reflects on fashion.

High on Rams Hill, two miles to the north, is a ploughed-down enclosure contemporary with Lambourn Seven Barrows, set at the side of the Ridge Way, and looking out over the Vale of White Horse to the Cotswold Hills. To the east of Seven Barrows is a disc-barrow on Nutwood Down and another on Mere End Down; to the west, a disc-barrow on the crest of Woolstone Down, the lovely smooth line of which runs down from White Horse Hill to Upper Lambourn. So the people of Stonehenge lived here, the Wessex Culture, and characteristically their remains spread over a wide area with a centre, in this case having no henge monument. One can picture them benefiting by trade and tribute from the traffic passing up the Ridge Way towards the crossing over the Thames at Streatley, to continue on along the Icknield Way to other Wessex Culture communities at Little Cressingham and Weasenham in Norfolk and on upwards to the Wash.

The thread running through this ancient world in Berkshire and joining it to the seat of power at Stonehenge is the Ridge Way. Distribution maps show that Stonehenge man travelled this way.

From near Wayland's Smithy, the Ridge Way looks like a white and green striated ribbon, dwindling and then disappearing from view over the crest by the rampart of Uffington Castle. Over the hills and far away – its drawing power is intense. From here Stonehenge man would have travelled up to the Wessex Culture kingdom in Norfolk. From Stonehenge, he would have travelled to Knowlton Circles and the Dorset coast by Dorchester; he would go down to the domains of the Wessex Culture chieftains in Cornwall and through the Frome Gap to the Mendips and Bristol Channel; he would journey up to North Wales and then perhaps across the sea to Ireland.

What can travel have been like to a Stonehenge man? The common man can have travelled very little except in attendance on his master. The power to travel was a perquisite of royalty and aristocracy and even then was attended with incessant danger. But this would not deter formidable men like Odysseus, whose personality and bearing could call forth the rules of aristocratic hospitality, and whose life as a warrior was in any case in peril of violent death from the cradle to the grave.

Telemachus, Odysseus' son, travels far across Greece seeking news of his father with just one companion, the royal son of Nestor. They arrive at the palace of Menelaus, brother of Agamemnon, and comrade in arms of Odysseus during the Trojan War.

'The two travellers, Prince Telemachus and Nestor's noble son, come to a standstill in their chariot at the courtyard gate.' An equerry goes in to Menelaus and says, 'May it please your majesty, we have some strangers here at the gates – a couple of men whom I take by their looks to be of royal blood.' Menelaus responds, 'Think of all the hospitality that you and I enjoyed from strangers before we reached our homes and could expect that Zeus might spare us from such pressing need again. Unyoke their horses at once, and bring our visitors into the house to join us at the feast.' They bathe and change their clothing and then Menelaus greets them, 'Fall to, and welcome. After you've dined we shall inquire who you may be. Your pedigree has left a stamp upon your looks that makes me take you for the sons of kings, those sceptred favourites of Zeus, for no mean folk could breed such men as you are.'[2]

The brotherhood of aristocracy would have bonded the warrior class of Stonehenge in such a way, making it no less likely that often they would be fighting each other to the death on a cattle raid, seeking booty and destruction in the respected tradition of the warrior. Telemachus' royal bearing was a passport into the palace of Menelaus, to be entertained by himself and his wife Helen, whose beauty was the cause of the Trojan War.

In the Ireland of Cu Chulainn, the ties of aristocracy were strengthened by the custom of fosterage, by which a lesser chief would place his son for upbringing with a greater, thereby creating a bond between their houses. The ties of regard between foster-brothers could be very strong, none the less often broken by later unavoidable combat giving such stories something of the power of Greek tragedy, as in the mutual love shown in the deadly combat between Cu Chulainn and Ferdia.

One cause of travel in Stonehenge Britain would be the seasonal festivals, when gifts of great value would be carried and exchanged for reasons of prestige and alliance. It is likely that this gift-giving accounts for much of the transference of valuable goods that appears in the archaeological record to be the result of commercial trade.

The segmented faience beads from the eastern Mediterranean have found their way up into Norfolk, and it is probable that they travelled there along the Ridge Way and Icknield Way in the possession of a Norfolk chieftain who had been given them as high prestige gifts by an overlord at Stonehenge, where the great concentration of these beads is found. He may have travelled during an annual period of truce to a great festival, which we know to be the case in Ireland from the written traditions there.

How such a long journey would be made is at present uncertain. From the actual archaeological remains found so far, it might seem that the journey would have been made on foot, irrespective of the importance of the person making it. Horse bones have been found mingled with other animal bones in the remains of the period, so the horse was present in Britain, but it may have been a wild animal hunted only for its food value. On the other hand, as it seems the ruling class were of Indo-European origin, one would have expected them to have the horse-drawn chariot, which was basic to their military power over much of Europe and Asia. Perhaps the skill and organisation in the complex craft of horse-training had been left behind temporarily in their migration across the sea from Europe. Much of the equipment of horse-harnessing is perishable and would not survive, but bits and cheek-pieces must be durable and those found must be dated to a late stage in the Bronze Age, after the

Wessex Culture had ended. This does not necessarily mean that they may not yet be found. The chariot for the use of a warrior ruling class would fit comprehensibly into the clearing picture of barbarian Stonehenge times. Solid wooden wheels indicating the use of wagons of some sort have been found from an earlier – Neolithic – date than this in bogs in Holland.

In Sweden, rock-carvings of Bronze Age life show the four-spoked wheel that was used by the Hittites and Mycenaeans for their earlier chariots.

Another possibility to ease the fatigue of a long journey for a highly self-regarding Wessex chieftain would be the litter. There is no evidence to suggest the use of this form of transport in Britain, but its materials would leave no remains, and in the absence of the trained horse, the possibility should not be ignored. It is difficult to visualise haughty warrior-kings with the power to build Stonehenge tramping mile after mile like any bondsman. A model and a fresco representing such litters in the Crete of 1800–1500 BC show that this form of transport was used in Europe at that time, and it is also attested on the mainland of Mycenaean Greece.

Inevitably, one's mind comes back to vehicles drawn by animals. The high level of the various skills shown in the building of Stonehenge make one doubt the absence of knowledge of the wheel, on which the presence of most vehicles depends. The horse existed in the Stonehenge world, and so did oxen in great numbers. That the haulage of the biggest sarsens of Stonehenge was done by manpower seems clear from the difficulty of mustering a concerted effort from a concourse of intractable oxen harnessed to a complex of cables attached to the stone. Ineffectual confusion would seem the inevitable result. Evidence from the Mediterranean shows that manpower was used for tasks calling for complicated organisation by the leaders and understanding from the massed performers.

On the other hand, it seems likely that with the great power-potential of the prospering herds that must have existed, many of the lesser haulage tasks for which small ox-teams would have been ideal – such as hauling smaller stones and heavy timber for rollers and sledges – were probably done by oxen.

The fresh problems raised by the unique task of building Stonehenge are just the sort of stimulants that lead to the birth of new techniques, and it could be from them that the first vehicles in Britain resulted. No doubt clearer evidence shedding light on this will come, but meanwhile it is fascinating to be able to walk along the Ridge Way, knowing that your steps cannot be far from following the royal progresses of kings of three and four thousand years ago.

The plover planed low in the wind then, as he does now, uttering his paean of the downs, and watched the noisy retinue of men go past, leaving the downs again in silence.

REFERENCES

1. Hoare, R. C., *Ancient Wiltshire*, 1819.
2. Homer (Trans. E. V. Rieu), *The Odyssey*, Penguin, 1946.

CHAPTER 13

The 'Stonehenge Language'

PERHAPS ONE of our greatest mental blockages regarding the Stonehenge people is that we do not know the language they spoke. Most periods of our history have had historical novels written about them, but not Stonehenge Britain. The human events suggested by the Bronze Age were not local; this is a period of our history quite as important to our understanding as Tudor England; if periods are comparable, perhaps more significant, with its sudden cultural uplift and pioneering of technology. Perhaps someone in the not far distant future will attempt to show at least the broad sweep of it in a historical novel. In my view, we are nearing a state of knowledge when this could be attempted, and if the facts were properly synthesised, necessarily leavened with imagination, it would be a gain to understanding.

I have myself thought on these lines, but the question of the Stonehenge language is a great technical difficulty in attempting to write of its world. Without language, what names can be given to individual people and places? The name Stonehenge, itself, is Anglo-Saxon, and is merely descriptive of hanging stones. It first appears in English literature in *Historia Anglorum*, written by Henry of Huntingdon about AD 1130. The name relates in no way to the original name given to it by its builders, which we do not know. The original name of the Stonehenge capital may have come from a king or a god or a geographic connexion of the time.

I once thought about this for a long time, and dabbled half-heartedly in the Celtic languages, in particular Old Irish as the oldest rooted of these. But to use Old Irish would be unjustifiable as archaeology suggests that Celtic language reached Ireland about the fifth century BC whereas Stonehenge was built about 1500 BC. What other possibilities are left? The classical writers recorded the

Caledonians who later it seems merged into the Picts. These people left inscriptions in a known script, that of ogham, but no one has succeeded in deciphering these – unlike the Celtic ogham inscriptions – as the language is not known. It was probably a non-Indo-European language, pre-dating Celtic in Britain. There is evidence that this language had existed, but as the language itself is unknown, it is of no assistance.

The only non-Indo-European language still spoken in western Europe is Basque of south-west France and northern Spain. The fact that it is pre-Indo-European guarantees its great antiquity, but does not link it necessarily to Stonehenge Britain. This really seems to exhaust all the possibilities, but the problem remains. In writing a historical novel of Stonehenge, what could one call the capital; what personal names for the king and other characters; what name for the River Avon and the Prescelly Mountains?

The last of these led me on a devious path. I am partly resident in Wales by the border near Hay-on-Wye. It is now a non-Welsh-speaking area but I use a Welsh dictionary to find the meanings of local place-names. I was looking at this dictionary just before retiring to bed one night, when the thought struck me to look up the meaning of the word 'Prescelly'. I turned to the first syllable and read, 'pres, n.m. brass; bronze; copper; money'. One word stood out from all the others, 'bronze'. This was a most amazing coincidence. A mountain that was thought to be sacred in the Bronze Age and its sacred nature to have been derived from being situated near the metal route to Ireland, had one meaning in English for its first syllable 'bronze'. To a non-philologist, the odds against this happening by chance seemed high. So I quickly turned back the pages and saw on a page which to me at that startling moment might otherwise have been blank, 'celi, Celi, n.m. heaven, God'.

I looked at the page in fixed amazement, almost disbelief, and the thought seriously crossed my mind whether I was in the midst of a dream. After all the years of research and thought about why the bluestones were brought from Prescelly to Stonehenge; a period giving rise to the belief that Prescelly was a sacred mountain by the metal route to Ireland; then this meaning seemed to stand out from the page in front of me – 'bronze god'. Was this like Professor Atkinson's chance discovery of the Stonehenge carvings again? In his case, millions of people had looked at the carvings unseeingly before him. On this basis, was it possible that no one had previously thought of a possible meaning of 'Prescelly'? I could not believe this, yet, knowing little of philology, the likelihood of chance operating on *two* syllables in this way seemed remote. If 'Prescelly' could be translated as 'bronze god', not only would this seem to confirm the supposed sacred nature of Mount Prescelly, but the possibility would arise that some form of the Indo-European languages had been used in naming it in Bronze Age times and that this name had persisted from then to the present day. It could mean that the language of Stonehenge Britain was a branch of Indo-European. If this were true it would be a major historical discovery with many ramifications into fields other than language.

Three and a half thousand years and more would be an extraordinary length of time for the name to have persisted unchanged, but given that there had been a radical change in language, this could still point to a persistence in folk-memory till the time of its present naming of the once great reverence for Prescelly, a reverence which had already been proposed from other evidence.

I alternated between a certainty that I had made an important discovery and an equal certainty that such a simple line of research could not have been overlooked. The chances seemed very great against the separate meaning of two syllables and their collective significance fitting an existing theory exactly. If this was coincidence, it was the exact coincidence of several factors, which could be correlated thus:

Existing Theory	*Phonetics of 'Prescelly'*
1. Metal route.	1. First syllable – bronze, copper.
2. Sacred mountain of god.	2. Second syllable – god.
	3. Meaningful collective word – bronze or copper god.

I thought of the part coincidence had played in the decipherment of the Mycenaean Linear B tablets, leading to its final acceptance. Ventris and his collaborator John Chadwick had already advanced the revolutionary thesis that Linear B was an early form of Greek (Sir Arthur Evans having said after years of study that whatever the language, it was *not* Greek), when Professor Blegne excavating Pylos, Nestor's palace in south-west Greece, found a new batch of Linear B tablets. Linear B is a syllabic script that includes at the end of the syllabic cyphers a stylised pictogram for the word written. In this case, tripods and pots with varying numbers of legs and handles were shown in the pictograms, and the numbers of legs and handles agreed with Ventris' translation of the script, as used by Blegen. He wrote a famous letter to Ventris, which virtually sealed the success of the decipherment. It ended, 'All this seems too good to be true. Is coincidence excluded?'[1]

Would coincidence be excluded with 'Prescelly'? I took action to find what the experts said.

I wrote to Professor R. J. C. Atkinson. He replied that in the course of his archaeological work on Stonehenge in the 1950s, he had consulted Sir Ifor Williams, the leading authority on Welsh place-names, who had given the derivation of 'Prescelly' from 'Pris(g)-Seleu', meaning in English 'Solomon's Bush'. Sir Ifor Williams did not attempt to explain this apparently Biblical name for a mountain in Wales. An alternative suggestion to Professor Atkinson had been from 'Pre-Seleu', meaning 'Solomon's Hill'.

I next wrote for an interview, kindly granted, with I. L. Foster, Professor of Celtic Languages at Oxford University, regarding both 'Prescelly' and the question of the Stonehenge language. He received me in his high-ceilinged, gracious rooms at Jesus College. First we dealt with the Stonehenge language, and I put forward my questions. At some of them he rose and went into an inner room, which seemed shelved with books almost from floor to high ceiling, and returned with his finger pointing at a paragraph that was the most authoritative answer to my query. I was reminded of a story of my stepfather who was a professor. A colleague of his referred to a book on being asked a question. A comment was made that he had referred to a book for the answer. He replied, 'The art of knowledge is in knowing that on a certain shelf, in a certain book, on a certain page, is the *correct* answer to any question.' And so Professor Foster directed my attention to all the right books to consult later, while giving me his most authoritative advice, for which I thank him.

Then I asked him the meaning of 'Prescelly'. His answer was the same as that of Sir Ifor Williams; 'Solomon's Bush' was reaffirmed.

The 'c' in 'Prescelly' is intrusive, it seems, as it does not appear in the earlier written forms of 'Presely' or 'Preseli', which lead towards 'Solomon's Bush', although the phonetics do not change. 'Pres', the Welsh word for 'bronze, copper', is related phonetically to the English word 'brass', from the Welsh practice of changing the sound of an English 'b' to 'p'; as Fluellen says in *Henry the Fifth*, 'All the water in Wye cannot wash your Majesty's Welsh plood out of your pody.' The date when Mount Prescelly was named is not known; it may have been at a later date when folk-memory – now forgotten – played its part. The answer may lie in the involutions of the earlier, unwritten Indo-European languages of northern Europe.

Before leaving the subject, I will say that the association of a god and bronze or copper would be a natural one in the days when metal was first beginning to place power in the hands of man. This may be shown in Cretan myth in the person of Talos, who has a double identity as the artificer-smith Daedalus' apprentice (who first invented compasses for inscribing circles), and as the bronze man forged by Hephaestus who circled Crete thrice daily for its protection. Hesychius gives Talos as a name for the Sun, and Talos' other name Circinus may refer both to compasses and to the circling of the sun. Some conception of an early artificer-Sun-God may lie in this myth from distant Crete.

The difficulty of the question of the language of Stonehenge Britain is still far from complete resolution. It is a problem which lies partly in the field of philology and partly in that of archaeology.

Philologists can only work in a medium providing some indication of language in the form of literature or inscriptions. If this is provided in even scanty form, such as the Linear B tablets, then a philological knowledge of the wider field of languages will fill in much of the picture. Archaeology is a science that by its nature examines the inanimate objects of people of the past, but cannot, again, re-create language in the absence of writing. But when philology and archaeology combine chains of possibilities can appear. The philologist can provide the language in a literate part of the world, and the archaeologist trace cultures leading from this area, which possibly bore the same language with them into illiterate parts.

The fact that many languages spoken between India in the east and Ireland in the west had features in common was commented on well over a century ago. Theories to account for this linguistic similarity of peoples thought previously to be widely separated in every respect have been numerous. What might appear to some a dry academic discussion suitable only to donnish common-rooms, blazed frighteningly to life in the world of action in the 1930s when turned to his purpose by Adolf Hitler. He distilled the often tentatively held views of many scholars, who had sought to clarify the expansion of the Indo-Europeans, into a creed of the innate superiority of the Germanic peoples, made none the less powerful in its appeal by the evocative mists enshrouding such ancient events. He enlivened the scholastic mists by peopling them with the Germanic gods of Wagner's operas. He unjustifiably equated the name of the Indo-European invaders of India, the Aryans, with other Indo-Europeans who probably inhabited Germany at this time, and mistakenly, in the opinion of most scholars, placed the focus of Indo-European expansion in Germany and not on the southern Russian steppes. By so doing, he gained for Nazi-ism the psychological reassurance of an ancestry which had spread victoriously across half the Europe-Asia land mass. The truth of scholarly research has been far different from this and the enormous problems of correlating the archaeological and linguistic evidence from this vast area have exercised scholars of many countries and for many years.

Possibly typical of the focus of the Indo-European spread are the chieftains' tombs of the Kuban River in the north Caucasus area. These great barrows had single burials under them in shafts not unlike the Shaft Graves at Mycenae, and were richly furnished with gold, copper and silver objects, precious stones, and elaborately patterned fabrics, still surviving astonishingly from about 2500 BC. The wheels of wagons are a recurring feature with these burials.

This barbarian area north of the Caucasus was non-literate, so the evidence here at the primary point in the trail is purely archaeological. The earliest literary evidence of the spread from here of peoples are the writings of the Hittites inscribed on stone and upon seals. The Hittites were an Oriental people, but in the first half of the second millennium BC aristocratic warriors in chariots and armed with battle-axes came from north of the Caucasus and became the ruling class of the country extending over much of Asia Minor and Syria whose power lasted from 2000–1200 BC. They built a great capital city, Hattusas, south of the Black Sea. In the general balance of political power during this period, the Hittites ranked only behind mighty Egypt and the Assyro-Babylonians in the affairs of the Middle East, and their archives tell us that in 1595 BC even Babylon itself was sacked by a Hittite army, spear-headed by chariots, and led by King Mursilis. Writing in a hieroglyphic script developed in this kingdom sometime before 1500 BC.

Professor Bedrich Hrozny of the Czech University, Prague, set out to solve the Hittite script in the period around 1913. In this he succeeded. A key sentence of his solution had an intrusive word in it known to him from another language, 'ninda', which he knew to mean 'bread'. He suspected that a word meaning 'water' might be associated with this and in the same sentence was the word 'vâdar'. This word did in fact prove eventually to be 'water'. The astonishing nature of the resemblance of the word 'vâdar' in an oriental language of the second millennium BC to the modern English word 'water' needs no elaborating, but as Professor Hrozny's researches continued he found that not only did many Hittite words resemble modern or old European words, but that the declensions were often almost precisely similar.

This first step in the linguistic trail of the Indo-Europeans was carried on to writings in ancient Persia and India and even beyond in Chinese Turkestan, and in a westerly direction to Greece. These places have writings which approximate in date to the time of Stonehenge, but literacy did not spread in this direction, so only archaeology can suggest the trail towards north-western Europe.

The trail of the Indo-European language across Europe is suggested by the spread of the practice of single-grave burial, resembling those burials we have mentioned in the Kuban River area of the north Caucasus. Accompanying this burial custom right across Europe to the Rhine and Holland is the appearance of pottery decorated by having cord pressed into it before it is fired and the placing of a battle-axe with the dead. A particular type of hammer-headed dress-pin also accompanies the trail as do small models of wagons, and the occurrence of wooden wheels in Holland, implying the spread of horse- and oxen-using people. Radio-carbon dates have been obtained of these makers of battle-axes and so-called Corded Ware in north-west Europe, and these begin about 2500 BC. This date is little different from that estimated for the Kuban burials so it is thought that this Indo-European spread must have been rapid. A rapid spread of this nature makes it quite possible that the Indo-European language of the north Caucasus was carried across Europe largely unchanged. Professor Stuart Piggott has written in 1965 in his book *Ancient Europe*, 'From the beginning of the second millennium BC we move without a substantial break into a central Europe that, by early in the first, can hardly be other than Celtic and perhaps Germanic-speaking. I would not say that our late third millennium emigrants from the south Russian steppes spoke Celtic, or Italic or Germanic or any other known Indo-European language of central or west Europe. But the likelihood that they did speak one or more dialects within the Indo-European group seems to me a very strong one.'[2]

We have seen the evidence of the crossing of the single-grave, battle-axe users into Britain early in the second millennium BC, in an earlier chapter. So it is on this archaeological, non-literary evidence that any supposition of the language of Stonehenge Britain must rest at the present time. In this distant, until recently almost completely fog-enshrouded, period, it is illuminating that the language may have been allied to the Indo-European languages familiar to us, and the occurrence of Hittite writings of this period so comparatively near to the source of the geographic spread of the Indo-Europeans, coupled with the rapidity of this spread to north-west Europe, does seem to bring the conception a little closer.

It would seem that the immigrating battle-axe users into Britain found an indigenous population speaking a language different from their own, and this language probably had its fundamental origins in the Mediterranean. One can picture then a Stonehenge Britain with an élite language for its rulers and another language for the mass of the people, as, say, in Anglo-Saxon England after the Norman Conquest, or as in the Hittite kingdom itself. As to what language the mass of the people of Stonehenge spoke, it seems that the only possible clue, and that an extremely tenuous one, might be provided by the Basque language.

The term Indo-European applies strictly only to language; none the less the focal origin, north of the Caucasus Mountains, argues some degree of racial homogeneity amongst these people. The Aryan invasion of northern India was seen by them as their fair-skinned race struggling against the dark-skinned indigenous population. Menelaus, brother of Agamemnon, in the *Iliad* from his description is of a non-Mediterranean type – huge and red-headed. The graves in Britain reveal the earlier slightly built Mediterranean physical type followed by a more robust, round-headed people. It is probably fair to equate this evidence with the general Indo-European picture and consider that the Stonehenge ruling class was broadly fairer-skinned and bigger-built than the people it dominated.

The enormous field of this archaeological and philological research ranging over all Europe and great areas of Asia means that, much as has been done to find the Indo-Europeans, there is far more left to do. As time goes on more and more light will be thrown on Stonehenge from these researches into the vaster field of the Indo-Europeans.

REFERENCES

1. Chadwick, John, *The Decipherment of Linear B*, Cambridge University Press, 1958.

2. Piggott, Stuart, *Ancient Europe*, Edinburgh University Press, 1965.

CHAPTER 14

Sea Trade

NEAR THE beginning of this book, I brought forward the opinions of the foremost authorities that Stonehenge was built by a Mycenaean, and that there was evidence of contact from the eastern Mediterranean with Britain in the form of the segmented faience beads. Later, we saw that Dr Glyn Daniel interpreted the archaeological evidence left by the Megalith Builders as that of metal prospecting and sea voyaging to north-west Europe, including the British Isles. We must differentiate between these two periods; that of the Megalith Builders being predominantly in the third millennium BC, and that of the heyday of Stonehenge and Mycenae being in the second millennium BC.

Let us look at the evidence of contacts between Stonehenge Britain and the Mediterranean, and that of ancient seamanship. On the first, we have already seen that of the supposedly Mycenaean dagger carving at Stonehenge and the faience beads. Another relevant find may be the Rillaton Gold Cup, now in the British Museum. This cup was found in 1818 in a large stone-built grave inserted in a round barrow on Bodmin Moor in Cornwall. With it were a bronze dagger, 'some pieces of ivory', and 'a few glass beads' (these may have been faience beads). It is a most handsome vessel but particular interest attaches to it as features in its gold design and workmanship are paralleled by cups belonging to heroic societies outside Britain – one from Fritzdorf in the Rhineland, and some from the Shaft Graves at Mycenae. Lord William Taylour writes in his book, *The Mycenaeans*, published in 1964, referring to one of the Mycenaean cups, '. . . a style of horizontal flutings was adopted. A similar technique was used on a gold cup found at Rillaton in Cornwall. The shape of the Rillaton is different but it is generally believed that it is actual Mycenaean work or an imitation of it.'

The Stonehenge dagger carving is not the only one in Britain. On a stone in a round barrow at Badbury in Dorset, similar daggers and axes were also carved, and further light may be shed by the finding of an actual Mycenaean sword-hilt in a barrow at Pelynt in south-east Cornwall. This sword dates from around 1300 BC, and Mycenaean authorities are agreed as to its origin.

As with the Rillaton Cup, this evidence from Cornwall, the land of tin, may be particularly significant.

A splendid type of object found in three Wiltshire barrows is the gold-bound amber disc. These are similar to one found in the Tomb of the Double Axes at Knossos. There has been uncertainty, if these do represent trade between the Aegean and Wessex, as to which originated the type, but the balance of recent opinion is that they were made in the Mediterranean and traded to Britain. It is a reflection on the activity of Bronze Age trade, if this is so, that the amber for the discs should have travelled from Jutland to southern Europe, and then for the discs to have eventually found a resting place in Britain.

Trade in the other direction is illustrated more clearly by ornaments of very specific design known as 'crescentric necklaces'. These were commonly made of amber and had in their design large spacer beads, pierced in a complex manner for stringing. They were very fashionable in Stonehenge Britain and have been found at Mycenae, Kakoratos and Pylos in Greece. Of the Greek examples Lord William Taylour has written '. . . these could well have borne the trade-mark Made in England.'[1]

We have looked at the sceptre with the burial in Bush Barrow near Stonehenge. The mounts for this have a zigzag or dentated outline. Exactly similar mounts were found in the Shaft Graves at Mycenae, with a wealth of ornamental inlays from furniture and of carved figures plainly made of ivory, and they are said to be of this material. The mounts of Bush Barrow are said to be of bone, but the distinction of aged ivory and bone is finely drawn.

In both Crete and Mycenaean Greece the double-axe is a recurrent symbol at the places of the greatest ritual significance, such as the shrines and royal palaces. It is carved symbolically in various materials at these places, and the actual implement or weapon, the labrys, made of copper or bronze, has been plentifully found. These are of a symmetrical shape with a central shaft-hole and an edged blade to either side. Four of these metal double-axes of thirteenth century BC date – one from Topsham, Devon – have been found in the British Isles and also a miniature pendant replica made in Kimmeridge shale. The four metal axes are probably tangible imports into Britain from the Aegean, but it is possible that some of the symbolism underlying the axe carvings at Stonehenge and Badbury was similarly imported into Britain in the minds of men, and expressed in the single-bladed native variety of axe.

An H-shaped ingot of tin, typical of the shape cast for transporting the raw material in the Mediterranean, has been found in Cornwall, but whether this is Bronze Age or later is difficult to determine. Ingots such as these may be an indication of purely commercial trade carried out by barter. With articles of prestige, however, such as those of adornment and weapons, their movement can be accounted for in part by the gifts passing between heroic leaders. In the *Odyssey*, for instance, as Telemachus prepares to leave Menelaus' palace, Menelaus says,

> 'You shall have the loveliest and most precious of the treasures that my palace holds. I'll give you a mixing-bowl of wrought metal. It is solid silver with a rim of gold round the top and was made by Hephaestus himself. I had it from my royal friend the King of Sidon, when I put up under his roof on my journey home. That is the present I should like you to take.'[2]

Menelaus in Sparta passes a precious mixing-bowl he has been given in Phoenicia to Telemachus who takes it to Ithaca off the west coast of Greece. The short account takes the bowl on a journey of nearly a thousand miles.

This, then, is some of the evidence that goods from the Aegean found their way to Britain, and in the reverse direction. How did they travel? Was it really through the voyages of ultra-daring seamen, or was Bronze Age seamanship more advanced than our imaginations tend to let us admit; perhaps as Mr Geoffrey Bibby visualises it, with distant voyaging, though hazardous, of an almost routine nature? Or is all this a mirage – simply not on the cards? After all, it is possible to imagine the goods travelling from hand to hand as Telemachus' cup did.

We know fully the dangers endured by ocean voyagers in historic times. Columbus' hazardous voyage took place late in the fifteenth century. Prince Henry of Portugal – so famed as a seaman that he was known as 'the Navigator' – did not succeed in his lifetime during the fifteenth century in sending ships beyond the Gambia River, a mere two thousand miles down the western coast of Africa.

Is it conceivable that three thousand years before this, the skill of shipbuilding, and knowledge of navigation could have been sufficiently advanced for ships to have plied other than on the tideless Inland Sea, the Mediterranean, where, by the use of known routes, a ship's captain need seldom be out of sight of land? North, beyond the Straits of Gibraltar, the Atlantic rollers of the Bay of Biscay are frequently whipped into gales and the tides cause tide-races and whirlpools by islands and headlands.

It must be remembered that in the Bronze Age there was one particular lure to explorers – tin. In order to produce bronze of the best properties, it must be alloyed of 90 per cent copper and 10 per cent tin. Copper is comparatively widespread, but tin is of rare occurrence. It is probable that Bohemia in central Europe, Spain, Brittany and Cornwall were the only sources available to the ancients. No specific Bronze Age workings have been identified in Cornwall, but the analysis of British bronze artifacts in recent years has shown that these frequently contain the ideal 10 per cent of tin – unlike those of other areas of northern Europe – showing that the Cornish deposits were almost certainly being used. In more primitive areas of Europe, copper might be hardened by alloying a small quantity of arsenic, but the rich civilisations of the Aegean had to have the best – Homer's 'unyielding bronze'.

Between the great days of Greek seafaring (and also those of the Phoenicians) and those of Henry the Navigator, in the fifteenth century, there lie the periods of the Roman Empire followed by the Dark Ages after the Empire collapsed. The Romans had untold wealth and the courage to explore the seas, but they were not a maritime people and lacked the imaginative zest of the Greeks. In the Dark Ages skills and knowledge were lost and had to be slowly built up again in the Middle Ages. So the rapid advances in seafaring made by the Greeks and Phoenicians were not carried on at the same pace in the centuries that followed their zeniths.

Other than the poetic language of *The Voyage of Argo*, and *The Odyssey*, we have no documentary record of voyaging referring to a time at all comparable with that of Stonehenge, but let us look at the earliest records that do exist.

Possibly the most revealing of these is in *The Histories*, by Herodotus, the Greek 'father of history', writing in the fifth century BC. The historic and geographic writings of Herodotus have been much doubted through the ages, but the increasing knowledge of modern times has shown that his historical observation was acute and honest. His geographic knowledge was wide, but was subject to the limitations of his age. In all things he was a seeker after truth, but even so he may have passed on information in which he, himself, had been misinformed.

With this assessment of Herodotus in mind, how are we to view his account that about the time 600–595 BC Phoenicians circumnavigated the whole African continent? He writes:

> 'As for Libya (Africa, P.C.), we know that it is washed on all sides by the sea except where it joins Asia, as was first demonstrated, so far as our knowledge goes, by the Egyptian king Neco, who, after calling off the construction of the canal between the Nile and the Arabian gulf, sent out a fleet manned by a Phoenician crew with orders to sail west-about and return to Egypt and the Mediterranean by way of the Straits of Gibraltar. The Phoenicians sailed from the Arabian gulf into the southern ocean, and every autumn put in at some convenient spot on the Libyan coast, sowed a patch of ground, and waited for next year's harvest. Then, having got their grain, they put to sea again, and after two full years rounded the Pillars of Heracles (Straits of Gibraltar, P.C.) in the course of the third, and returned to Egypt. These men made a statement which I do not myself believe, though others may, to the effect that as they sailed on a westerly course round the southern end of Libya, they had the sun on their right – to northward of them. This is how Libya was first discovered to be surrounded by sea . . .'[3]

On the face of it, if it were not for the high reputation of Herodotus, this story could be dismissed out of hand, as such a voyage would be incredible. We have seen that at near the beginning of modern times in the fifteenth century, Henry the Navigator had only succeeded in exploring two thousand miles down the west coast of Africa, whereas the circumnavigation of the continent would be in the region of 13,500 miles. However, there is one feature in the tale which Herodotus would not accept, that the sun shone on the seamen's right hand when rounding the southern end of Africa. The honest scepticism of Herodotus paradoxically reinforces our view of the tale to the point of belief, as we know – as he did not –

that in fact the sun in the southern hemisphere would have been on the mariners' right hand, when sailing a westerly course. We can assume that Herodotus' source of the story of the voyage was one likely to be reliable or he would not have reported it, as he does, with acceptance, with reservation only on this point of the bearing of the sun, which in fact tends to be corroborative.

There can be no absolute certainty that this voyage was made, but many scholars believe that it was, and it does at least seem certain that the Phoenicians sailed into the southern hemisphere in the sixth century BC.

Tales such as these led to a sort of 'Phoenicomania' through which nearly all great voyages of antiquity were attributed to these people, but when the evidence is carefully sifted, the fact remains that the Phoenicians were among the most determined and successful seamen the world has known. The success appears in the stories of some of their voyages but their extreme secrecy about trade routes to ensure their monopoly of them has led to our knowledge of their seamanship being mostly derived from such non-Phoenicians as chose to write about them. This is the paradox: that the Phoenicians took an important part in the birth of the alphabet and yet have left few records of themselves. Even so, the earliest recorded sea-voyage, which was in the time of the Pharaoh named Snefru, about 3200 BC, took place between Egypt and Byblus in Phoenicia, with the 'bringing of 40 ships of 100 cubits with cedar wood', and it is probable that the Phoenicians themselves began to take an active part in this trade at an early date. Indeed, it is possible that the 'Byblus ship' was not Egyptian but Phoenician.

The Phoenicians later opened up the western Mediterranean, establishing colonies on the north African seaboard and in Spain. Gades, the modern Cadiz, was colonised by them it is thought about 1100 BC, and was then the great trading station both for Spanish metals and possibly for those from Brittany and Britain also. The famous native kingdom and port of Tartessus lay a short way to the north of Gades and this figures in the records of voyaging as one of the main outlets of Spanish metals and is the intermediary link between the peoples of the Mediterranean and Brittany, Cornwall and Ireland, the metal lands of the north. It is probable that the Phoenician 'Tarshish ships' of the Old Testament were the treasure ships returning from Tartessus.

Much later, Strabo, the Greek geographer, recorded in the first century BC that Phoenicians were voyaging from Gades via Corunna to the Tin Islands (possibly a depot in the Scilly Isles, or Cornwall itself). Phoenician voyaging to this destination would have started long before this date, but his account might infer that the voyages were direct across the Bay of Biscay, ignoring Brittany – the open ocean route. One would hesitate to say that the Phoenicians were not capable even of this; hazardous, frighteningly dangerous though it was, the Phoenicians seemed capable of driving themselves anywhere they heard of, if there was a big profit in it.

But the Phoenicians were not the only skilled seamen. The earliest literary reference to Britain – the first time that Britain moves out of utter prehistory because of the written word – resulted from the voyage of a Greek captain in the sixth century BC. At this time the Greeks had a great trading colony at Massilia, the modern Marseilles. The Massilian captain voyaged north beyond the Straits of Gibraltar and wrote a Periplus (or Sailing Direction) of the voyage about 525 BC. The original document is lost but a garbled version survives in a poem by Avienus of the fourth century AD which reads:

'But hence (from Brittany) in two suns' time a boat
May travel to the Sacred Isle (Ireland):
(Thus 'twas yclept by men of old)
It lieth in betwixt the waves,
And occupieth many acres.
And in it roomily resideth
The folk of the Hibernians
And eke hard by there stretcheth out
The isle of the Albiones.'[4]

At this time Britain was called Albion, a name to be changed not very long after to a form resembling its present one. The Periplus stated or implied that the chain of trade was a shipping of goods from Britain and Ireland by the merchants of Oestrymnis (Brittany). Thence they were carried in the ships of the Tartessians of Spain, and then taken into the Mediterranean by Greek ships from Marseilles.

About 320 BC, one of the greatest voyages of antiquity was carried out by the Greek, Pytheas, again from Massilia. The voyage ranks high in the record of exploration of all time both for prowess and observation. Pytheas succeeded in breaking through the blockade of the Phoenicians and followed the west European coastline to

Brittany. From here he crossed to Cornwall near Land's End. Of this he writes:

> 'The inhabitants of Britain who dwell about the promontory known as Belerium are especially hospitable to strangers and have adopted a civilised manner of life because of their intercourse with merchants of other peoples. They it is who work the tin, treating the bed which bears it in an ingenious manner. This bed, being like rock, contains earthy seams and in them the workers quarry the ore, which they then melt down and cleanse of its impurities. Then they work the tin into pieces the size of knuckle-bones and convey it to an island which lies off Britain and is called Ictis (St Michael's Mount, P.C.); for at the time of ebb-tide the space between this island and the mainland becomes dry and they can take the tin in large quantities over to the island on their wagons.'[5]

The detailed nature of Pytheas' powers of observation can be seen in this extract, and he not only employed them in exploring inland in Britain on foot but by circumnavigating the whole island and reporting on an unknown land to the north, probably Norway. He then sailed to an island of amber to the east which was probably Heligoland. The comparatively detailed nature of his account with his reckonings of the distances he covered makes it virtually certain that he did indeed carry out this great voyage. His reckonings are overestimated but are consistent with the scale of overestimations invariably arrived at by dead reckoning by all mariners of his time.

These documentary accounts of early voyaging give a context, but do not extend to Stonehenge times. It is noteworthy, however, that some of the commodities for which seamen voyaged in these accounts were similar to those found in distant parts of Stonehenge Britain, particularly metals and amber.

We have no documentary records of voyaging in the Stonehenge period – but what can be found in the archaeological record? In this, there is far more than might be hoped for, or expected.

In the clay shore of the River Humber at North Ferriby in Yorkshire, the remnants of three superbly built ships have been found, the oldest of them producing material dated recently by the radio-carbon method to about 1500 BC – the heyday of Stonehenge. I use the word 'ships' deliberately, as the most complete example is estimated at 51·7 feet in length and 8·55 feet in breadth – in the context of Odysseus' Europe undoubtedly qualifying as a ship and not a boat. They were plank-built, the planks being jointed by expert and most intricate carpentry, and caulked and sewn.

It could be argued that these skilfully built ships came from overseas. I see no reason for this. Stonehenge Britain reveals many accomplishments (as an instance, its fine metalwork). Why not expert shipbuilding? Further, the three ships were found together with evidence suggesting a made-up trackway from the shore. The trees for the various different types of wood used to build the ships all appear in Yorkshire. In the absence of contradictory evidence, there is no reason to think that these ships were not native-built and operated. The three appear to have been in various stages of repair at a riverside settlement, where the chances of nature have preserved them in the clay.

Fig. D. Detail of skilful carpentry in North Ferriby ship, reflecting on second millenium carpentry as a whole.

The fact that there are three ships of similar and most distinctive design suggests that this type of ship may have been traditional elsewhere in Britain; in fact, that we may have here the typical ship of Stonehenge Britain – so different from concepts of water travel limited to skin-boats, coracles and dug-out canoes. Here is a solidly constructed ship, made rigid with elaborate jointing, and built of heavy timber planking. It was flat-bottomed, and so it was not ideally buoyant for sea-voyaging, but for strength and size it was a suitable craft for voyaging in fair weather. By the use of such a craft, coastal voyaging and voyaging from Britain to Europe remains hazardous, but to experienced seamen not unreasonably so.

I must digress from shipbuilding here to point out that this is one of the few instances of a specimen of the capabilities of Bronze Age carpenters being preserved by a chance of nature. We can see that the work is of a high standard of design and execution. This must reflect on the standard of construction of the timber buildings of barbarian Britain, which time has obliterated other than their post-holes. After studying the North Ferriby vessels, one should hesitate before limiting the potential excellence of the construction of such major buildings as Woodhenge. A plank for the bottom of one of the vessels is thirty-four feet long, with skilfully designed cleats incorporated in its working. Timber has been worked here skilfully and imaginatively almost to the limit of size of large tree-trunks. On the other hand, the more detailed work is of a high order.

Returning to ships: there is other evidence of the existence of ships in northern Europe in the Bronze Age. In Bohuslan, Sweden, are many outcropping rocks carved with men brandishing characteristic Bronze Age axes, and also ship-carvings, which, stylised as they are, may represent ships not dissimilar from the North Ferriby ships when these latter were complete. The carvings show an up-curving line fore and aft, similar to the North Ferriby vessels, embellished above by a great carved prow and stern-work. Many stylised men are shown in them, suggesting potential oar-power. Carvings possibly indicating a mast and sail also occur.

The dating of the Swedish ship-carvings is strengthened by a bronze sword found in Denmark which is engraved with similar ships. The sword can be dated to about 1500 BC. The possible affinities between the North Ferriby vessels and the Swedish rock-carvings (which may have fathered craft-designs found centuries later) may infer that this was a general design of ships in northern Europe.

With this potential of native, north European voyaging in the Bronze Age, there is less necessity to picture Stonehenge society sitting passively at home, while seamen from more advanced lands carried out the transference of luxury goods shown in the archaeological record. We know that Pytheas was not the first Mediterranean captain to voyage to the British Isles, and there is no reason therefore to assume that the Massilian voyage of about 525 BC was therefore the earliest. We do have these documentary proofs of very early voyaging in northern waters from the Mediterranean, but there is good cause with the North Ferriby vessels and Swedish rock-carvings to visualise, also, comparatively busy native voyaging.

What would be the purpose and incentive for such voyaging from

Britain? It is natural for people by the sea to have vessels for a number of purposes, but the primary one need not be peaceful trade. It has often been suggested that the Stonehenge capital of Britain acquired its wealth by the good fortune of lying on a natural, trans-peninsular route from the Bristol Channel to the English, between Ireland and north-west Europe. This conception could presuppose an unnecessarily passive role in the politics of the day. Elizabethan Britain looked and fought outside Britain for its wealth and supreme inspiration. Stonehenge Britain seems to have had societies equally inspired to dynamic action by its leaders from its evidence of talent and wealth. Our name for them – the Wessex Culture – how dead it sounds!

I see these north-European ships being used mainly for the purposes that heroic epic makes clear to us – marauding and sea-crossings for purposes of state. I do not see this on any great scale, but sufficient to produce the movement of luxury goods evident in northern Europe. I do not visualise the builders of the Stonehenge capitals and owners of their buried wealth sitting clod-like hoping for trading fortune to drop into their laps. I see them going out to procure such wealth as did not gravitate to their nodes of power as gifts from other equally mobile aristocratic barbarians.

Perhaps it was in the days of the Phoenicians that any large scale conceptions of trade as such in northern Europe were formalised. Even so they were also days of sacking and pillage, and with Menelaus' gift of the precious gold-rimmed cup to Telemachus in the days of the sacking of Troy in mind, perhaps it is more in the light of these human exchanges – pillage and gifts – that what appears to us as trade, including sea-trade, in the archaeological record should really be seen.

REFERENCES

1. Taylour, William, *The Mycenaeans*, Thames and Hudson, 1964.

2. Homer (Trans. E. V. Rieu), *The Odyssey*, Penguin, 1946.

3. Herodotus (Trans. Aubrey de Sélincourt), *The Histories*, Penguin, 1954.

4. Avienus, Festus Rufus, *Avieni ora maritima*, trans. in *The Ancient Explorers*, M. Cary and E. H. Warmington, Methuen, 1929, refer Ernst Adolf Schulten, Barcinone, 1922.

5. Diodorus Siculus (Trans. C. H. Oldfather), *Bibliotheca historica*, Loeb Classical Library, 1939.

CHAPTER 15

Controversy and Stonehenge the Building

PALACE? TEMPLE? Fort? Computer? Calendar? What is Stonehenge itself, the building? This book is concerned with Stonehenge people, but their finest surviving monument remains the greatest mystery of their time, made perhaps none the less mysterious by the heated controversy of savants at the present. Following the frequently wild speculation of centuries, for many years research on Stonehenge has proceeded in completely quiet waters. The interested general public has been vaguely aware that skilled investigation has been going on, and has been prepared to accept placidly the publication of fresh factual knowledge of Stonehenge, and such reserved interpretations as archaeologists have brought forward. How different the atmosphere, both learned and general, has suddenly become. A wave of theorising and speculation has swept in, starting from the astronomical knowledge of Professor Gerald S. Hawkins, of Boston University, U.S.A., being applied to the monument and his findings appearing in popular form in his book *Stonehenge Decoded.* A measure of the resulting controversy is the statement by Professor R. J. C. Atkinson, the archaeologist who has worked on Stonehenge for five seasons, that Professor Hawkins' book is 'tendentious, arrogant, slipshod and unconvincing'.

Professor Fred Hoyle, the Cambridge astronomer, has entered the arena and produced an alternative theory covering some of the same structural elements of Stonehenge. The situation is that eminent astronomers have new theories about Stonehenge; equally eminent archaeologists are doubtful if not condemnatory of much if not all of the astronomers' theorising. The argument has exploded out of the pages of journals into the newspapers on both sides of the Atlantic. It is a new and interesting situation in that scientists outside archaeology by applying their own specialised knowledge, astronomy, to Stonehenge are not only satisfied that their facts fit the monument, but from this they are moving into the field of the archaeologist and attempting to interpret the purpose and use of Stonehenge.

Professor Hawkins has several theses:

1. To a mean accuracy of under one degree, twelve of the significant stone alignments at Stonehenge point to an extreme position of the sun, and to a mean accuracy of about a degree and a half, twelve alignments point to an extreme position of the moon.
2. An eclipse of sun or moon always occurs when the winter moon rises over the Heel Stone. He states that not more than half these eclipses were visible from Stonehenge.
3. That when the winter moon swung over stone-hole D or F at Stonehenge, the harvest moon was eclipsed that year. This occurred in cycles of 19+19+18 years, giving a predictable eclipse every 56 years. This number, 56, corresponds with that of the number of Aubrey Holes, and by progressively moving around marker stones in these, one hole annually, such celestial events could be predicted, thus using the Aubrey Holes as a computer.

Hawkins points out that the occurrence of the approximately nineteen-year cycle may be noteworthy as Diodorus Siculus, the historian of the first century BC, speaks of a 'spherical temple' of the Hyperboreans (dwellers beyond the north wind) who live on an island (Britain?) which is visited by Apollo every nineteen years.

He puts forward the opinion that Stonehenge fulfilled the function of a calendar, which would be particularly useful for fixing the time to plant crops; and that it was an instrument of priestly power used to impress the multitude with knowledge of celestial phenomena.

Professor Hoyle supports some of Hawkins' astronomical findings, and further suggests that Stonehenge was capable of predicting virtually all eclipses. He also theorises that if the sun and moon were gods, their eclipse might suggest a third and more powerful god; that perhaps the all-powerful God, the God of Isaiah, had its origins in this way, and also the conception of the Trinity.

Professor Atkinson objects to a number of aspects of Hawkins' book. He points to several elementary inaccuracies in its earlier, archaeological chapters, such as the misstatement that swords and spears appear in Beaker graves. He says that some of the errors in alignment listed by Hawkins, far from being small, are of considerable dimension, and he considers the margin of two degrees Hawkins allows himself too great to prove significant. Hoyle writes that apparent errors could have been intentional on the part of the builders (this *could* be true, but in the immediate situation it seems strained reasoning).

Atkinson questions whether a barbarous and illiterate people who have left no evidence of numeracy could have designed Stonehenge to conform to such intricate astronomical data, particularly as the cycles of fifty-six years would have to be recognised over several generations. Other points he raises are that Hawkins has disregarded in his vertical readings the changes caused by the eroding of the ground surface by $1\frac{1}{2}$ feet since Stonehenge days, and that Hawkins has worked from plans of Stonehenge intended for illustrative purposes and not for scientific scaling.

A matter to which Professor Atkinson takes strong objection is that Professor Hawkins raises the possibility that stones at Stonehenge re-erected in recent times may have been replaced in changed positions, thereby not conforming to his expectations of alignment. As Professor Atkinson was concerned in this work carried out by the Ministry of Public Buildings and Works, and says that the stones were fitted with care into their former accurate moulds left in the soft chalk, this has been one of the major points causing the controversy.

I think that one point should be made clear: not all Professor Hawkins' sightings are geometrically exact lines (or as nearly exact as irregular holes and stones will allow) between two features. A number are made from the viewing of the sky from inside the monument through pairs of gaps aligned arbitrarily between the uprights of the trilithons and sarsen circle. A considerable width of the sky can be seen through these gaps, and the attaching of significance to celestial phenomena occurring in such wide areas of sky from quite arbitrary viewpoints seems questionable.

Hawkins' use of a computer for his calculations is of course irrelevant to the results obtained. While Stonehenge is laid out with considerable exactitude for a prehistoric building, by the nature of the irregular shape of many of the stones and holes in question, the exactness of the data fed into the computer is far removed from say the points and lines of a Euclid theorem. In other words, the computer, with all its accuracy, has no power over the exactness of the data with which it is fed, which none the less affects the validity of the results obtained.

It will have been seen that while Professor Hawkins has stimulated much fresh thinking, his theories are being seriously questioned. Shots between the heavy guns (Dr Glyn Daniel of Cambridge is also critical from the archaeological viewpoint) may have only started to be exchanged. More important than the controversy is the truth, and this may be a long time coming. Confidence in Professor Hawkins' theories is lessened by the working hypothesis on which he based his research, which was that if he could see any alignment, general relationship or use for the various parts of Stonehenge then these facts were also known to the builders. This hypothesis is by no means necessarily true.

A name which is constantly appearing in all the recent writings on this subject is that of Mr C. A. Newham. He is an amateur astronomer of Yorkshire. Somewhat earlier than Professor Hawkins, he had pointed to a far more limited but more specific set of astronomical alignments at Stonehenge, first in the *Yorkshire Post* and then in his booklet *The Enigma of Stonehenge*. His factual presentation is impressive, as is his avoidance of theorising.

In addition to his astronomical findings, Newham stated that at least nine linear measurements at Stonehenge corresponded in round numbers with the use of the unit of length, the Ancient Greek foot, employing this as being of 12·1608 modern English inches. For instance, from the centre of the Heel Stone, that significant outlier, to Aubrey Hole No. 28 at the far other end of the monument measured 400 Ancient Greek feet, and a quarter chord of the Aubrey Hole circle measured 200 Ancient Greek feet. The Ancient Greek foot is given in *Historical Metrology* by A. E. Berriman, the standard work on the subject, as 12·15 inches, although the figure of 12·16 inches is also mentioned. This is calculated from data from the ancient world and comparison with the known Roman foot. The best evidence for the Greek unit is the measurement of the platform of the Parthenon at Athens which is 100 Ancient Greek feet in width and 225 Ancient Greek feet in length.

The discrepancies of Newham's and other interpretations of the Ancient Greek foot are minute, and, disregarding this, it is to say the least surprising that the Parthenon of classical Greece and Stonehenge seem to have been laid out using the same unit of length. This further link to the Greek world increases one's respect for the builders of Stonehenge, and appears to project a certain unity of thought back into ancient Europe. Were the worlds of Mycenae and northern Europe so completely divorced and dissimilar?

Suddenly a spate of new facts regarding Stonehenge are flooding in from sources outside archaeology. When they are facts, such as some astronomical alignments and Newham's measurements appear, they may be steps towards the understanding of Stonehenge Britain. But archaeologists have absorbed a lesson from their own past. It does not do to speculate and interpret far beyond the facts. Two hundred years ago, William Stukeley in his later, highly imaginative years, set such a maelstrom of Near Eastern, Greek and Biblical fantasia whirling into the interpretation of our prehistoric monuments in Britain, as left a legacy right into the present century, that archaeologists now are rightly cautious. Progress is made by the recovery of clear evidence, and I do not foresee the intrusion of the God of Isaiah into prehistoric Britain being viewed with any favour by archaeologists, or contributing towards our true understanding of it.

The work of Sir Norman Lockyer in 1901 established that the entrance of the later Stonehenge is aligned as far as can be ascertained on to the rising sun of midsummer, and this could point to a fixing of the seasons by Stonehenge people. But I think that a large number of celestial alignments in a generally radial building such as Stonehenge, even allowing for certain apparently significantly placed stones and markers, should be viewed with caution. When there are so many points between which to align, it could be inevitable that many celestial events occur on some of the projections. There is no completely certain evidence that Stonehenge always had the open, unimpeded structure that its ruin presents now.

The question has frequently been asked: Was Stonehenge roofed? The question has usually been put and answered in the past relating to the standing stones, meaning: Did a roof cover the central stone structures at Stonehenge? Architecturally, this seems an impossibility due to the varying heights of the trilithons and the sarsen circle. No plausible plan can be devised to accommodate the height range of about 16 feet for the sarsen circle, through the intermediate heights of the paired trilithons of 20 feet and 21½ feet, to the Great Trilithon at 24 feet.

Clickhimin has introduced possibilities of totally new architectural concepts into prehistoric Britain, and as Stonehenge reduced to its simplest design of the circular bank and ditch and the inner sarsen circle conforms to the form of circularity common to all relevant structures of Late Neolithic and Bronze Age Britain, it would be as well to examine it from this point of view. This would mean regarding the structure as a whole and considering the possibility that the sarsen circle enclosed an open central courtyard with the five trilithons standing free in it, and that a radial, circular building similar to Woodhenge occupied the space from the sarsen circle out to the bank and ditch. Superficially this has attractions, and the eye is caught by the circles of so-called Y and Z holes set roughly concentrically outside the sarsen circle. These combined with the Aubrey Holes, travelling outward to the bank and ditch, seem to produce nebulous architectural concepts of a composite palace or fort of stone and timber, with the Aubrey Holes supporting the structure of the outer rampart. The cremations present in the Aubrey Holes would not be inconsistent with this concept as burials are common against the foot of structures in the period.

This architectural concept has many superficial attractions, not least that ignoring questions of detailed archaeological evidence and precise details of architectural support and structure, it would produce a feasible architectural plan fitting in very broad outline the ruin now standing at Stonehenge. It would change Stonehenge from a completely puzzling architectural anomaly to a palace structure.

But I am sure that the secrets of Stonehenge, the building, will have to be fought for up to the bitter end. After Clickhimin, such a solution as outlined could seem a feasible possibility, if such architectural details are ignored as that no ring of holes has been found between the Y holes and the Aubrey Holes, a distance to over-span in this conception of fifty to sixty feet.

The archaeological evidence is entirely against any such architectural concept. Professors Atkinson and Piggott and Dr Stone found no sign of any structure having been present in the Aubrey and Y and Z holes. They interpreted the Aubrey Holes and bank and ditch as having been made some centuries before the sarsen structure, and because the Y and Z holes correspond in number with the available bluestones, they considered that these had been dug to accommodate the bluestones, but that a change of plan led to the holes not being used and silting up gradually.

It is possible that these two apparently irreconcilable ways of viewing the evidence, architectural and archaeological, could in a sense be reconciled. The evidence is that operations were being undertaken at Stonehenge for a number of centuries, and that there were many changes in structure and even of plan in the course of execution. In the Irish myths, which I consider in their deeper layers have relevance to the Stonehenge world, great weight was attached to the reading of omens by the druids in most undertakings. It would be possible to visualise the digging of the bank and ditch as the first move towards establishing a conventional structure such as the Irish ring-forts, which Mr Hamilton sees in general as containing circular buildings. As often happens at the present day when planning by committee, the original plan may not have been carried through, and the structure may have continued to evolve, adapting itself to varying needs of ceremonial, tempered by indecision, and finishing as a completely unique structure, an anomalous hotch-potch, the result of many years' vacillation in dealing with a building of supreme public importance.

The upshot of all this is that Stonehenge itself still remains the supreme mystery – mysterious in almost all its aspects as a building. The veil has lifted considerably from its people and some other buildings of its time, but the more hard-won fact concerning Stonehenge that is gained, the deeper if anything, becomes the mystery. Professor Atkinson interprets it as primarily a temple, a structure in which to contact extra-mundane forces. By its nature, its ceremonial purpose seems clear.

The current furore may have added little that is concrete to the interpretation of Stonehenge so far (except perhaps the laying out in Ancient Greek feet advanced by Newham), but it has quickened the interest of many talented minds, and if there had been any sense of resignation to the fact that the purpose and use of Stonehenge would never be known for certain, this must surely have been swept away in a great wave of expectancy and interest. The friction of acute minds may quite suddenly at any time spark the answer to one of the most important problems of ancient history.

An extraordinary factor is that not one of the classical writers makes any clear reference to Stonehenge, not even at the time of the Roman conquest of Britain, when, assuming that the building was deserted and ruined, its outstanding nature would be expected to call forth some brief mention from contemporary writers. A point here might be that Stonehenge by its enduring nature may loom over-large in our assessment of the times. If Hamilton's postulation of large tribal forts in Britain is correct, we may have underestimated the scale of architecture that greeted Roman eyes in Britain, and with numerous other large buildings, the undoubted impressiveness of Stonehenge would have seemed relatively diminished.

Quite large amounts of Iron Age and Romano-British pottery have been found at Stonehenge, particularly in the Y and Z holes. The latter could be accounted for by Romano-British sightseers and so on, but I think it not inconceivable that Stonehenge may still have flourished on a diminished scale for such ceremonies as inauguration feasts of the local chieftains who continued their office in the time when Britain was in the Roman Empire. It is in this sort of ceremony and in the seasonal festivals presided over by the king that I see the function of Stonehenge; the magic of kingship being expressed, underlaid by the secondary power of priests and wise men. Certainly if the presence of Romano-British pottery is to be explained by any form of gathering, it could not at that period be connected with exclusively religious gatherings and the druids, as druidism was firmly stamped out by the Romans. It may be possible then that the continuance of archaic custom connected with local kingship went on with little comment in the Roman world on Salisbury Plain, at a time when the centres of real power had moved eastward and elsewhere. If this were true it would suggest that Stonehenge had never been a place of supreme priestly power and learning but a long accepted place of kingly ceremonial among its people. The qualities of magic and primitive religion would not be absent from such a conception, but it suggests ritual directed towards propitiation and observance for the most practical reasons, such as the well-being and prospering power of the whole people expressed through the king, and not so much an esoteric power resting in the hands of a priesthood.

I think that the trend of thought after the Clickhimin excavation will be away from a Stonehenge world obsessed with religion towards a world adapted to the everyday needs of man, but nothing so far points to Stonehenge itself being a utilitarian building, and I think that in its heyday it was the focus in the Stonehenge capital at which the people of southern Britain convened and through a seasonal peaceful assembly expressed overlordship and power, the law of the land, the basic common culture of all, in spite of differences, and the magic of the stable, fruitful elements in their lives, the food, the rivers, the land itself on which they lived – a religious yet practical gathering.

In Ireland, there are accounts still extant in the annals of the reasons for holding assemblies and what took place. That of Carmun in Leinster is the most detailed, although from the texts typical of the others. As is usual in ancient Ireland, the centre of Carmun was named after its female founder who died there, and one of the primary purposes of the assembly was as a wake for her, and to hold her funeral games once again in the form of chariot, horse and other races.

It was essential that kings, nobles and the whole people should attend.

> 'There comes for neglect of it
> baldness, weakness, early greyness,
> kings without keenness or jollity,
> without hospitality or truth.'

Hospitality and truth of a certain sort were fundamental qualities required of an ancient Irish king, qualities through which the prosperity of his people were expressed.

The assembly was a time of peace and friendship, any deed of violence being punished by death. The people went back to the lore of their beginnings, when the Tuatha De Danann, those most ancient and divine people, came to raise the first wailing over the dead Carmun and the first assembly was held, and the people recalled the hundreds of times the assembly had been held since. Declamations were made invoking the whole known lore of the land, battles, powerful teachings, the tales of other great feasts, topographical lore and divisions of the land, invasions, definitions of estates, great kings – the whole world known to the people was invoked.

Great importance was given to correct precedence at the assembly, and it was the occasion for granting new ranks.

Poets and men of other talents performed before the king, and he honoured them according to their quality.

The holding of the assembly was the occasion for the enactment of new laws and the settling of dues and tributes.

The successful holding of the assembly brought abundance of corn, milk, fruit, and fish in the lakes and rivers. It brought comfort in every house, the enjoyment of righteous laws, and freedom from conquest.

The tenor of the thought of the people regarding the Carmun Assembly can be seen in this detailed description and in the underlying fertility magic ensuing from a successful gathering held under a prospering king, and by the tribute paid to an entity appearing to be a nature goddess. The whole of an assembly would be greater than its parts. A psychological impulse of vigour, determination and unity would flow through the tribe from the holding of it with their king of strength, plenty, justice and truth.

It may be that here we have the description of similar events which took place at the Stonehenge capital, centring on perhaps the most enigmatic building in the world – Stonehenge. I see it as the fit setting for a king to perform his practical and magical ceremonial functions. Perhaps advanced astronomy played some part. If so, I think that much stronger evidence will have to be produced than at present. Recent astronomical theories have received the widest publicity, including presentation on television in America and Britain. We must guard against the possibility that a glamorous red herring may have been drawn across the trail to the Stonehenge people; that what may prove to be in great part invalid, may become an enduring part of folk-lore.

CHAPTER 16

Temple – or Home?

IN 1963, Mr Humphrey Case of the Ashmolean Museum, Oxford, made the following observation about some henge monuments excavated at Dorchester, Oxfordshire. 'The primary use is at least as likely to have been connected with settlement as with ceremonial.'[1] Settlement or ceremonial?

Instead of classifying these specific monuments as 'henges', as was done by the actual excavators, he prefers to use a more general term to embrace them, namely, 'ring-ditches'. Large numbers of these ring-ditches – well over 400 – have been recorded by aerial photography in the Oxford region alone. They are circular in shape, and commonly cannot be detected on the ground. They show up from the air usually through the more luxuriant growth over the deeper humus in their ditches producing a 'crop-mark', a circular shape of higher or greener growth. Their circular shape being reminiscent of a round barrow has led to a general assumption that they are ploughed out barrows, or burial places of a rudimentary form defined by a circular ditch. The most common type has signs that an outer bank once existed, making this type similar in this respect to a disc-barrow.

The balance of emphasis of interpretation by excavators of the round structures of the nature of round barrows has always been very heavily on the side of ceremonial, burial, and ritual. Such things as the posture of inhumation, the rites of cremation, the ritual significance of grave-goods have been revealed and discussed in an attempt to re-create the ritual of interment. Mr Case concluded his comments on some other ring-ditches at Stanton Harcourt, Oxfordshire, by saying, 'Might it not be therefore that we have here a settlement-complex of Late Neolithic semi-nomadic pastoralists . . . ?'[2] This sort of question was virtually never posed by the old antiquaries and has seldom been asked in recent times.

A notable exception was Professor V. Gordon Childe who in 1949 put forward the view that ring-ditches may have been built for habitation. But the unusual nature of Mr Case's comments may be gauged from the fact that the actual excavator at Stanton Harcourt, Miss Ann Hamlin, discusses the possible implications of ritual there without raising the possibility of this being a habitation site. The attractions of interpretations of ritual against those of everyday life are put concisely in Mr L. V. Grinsell's Glossary in his *The Archaeology of Wessex*. He writes: ' "Ritual Pit". Any pit found by archaeologists, the purpose of which is not evident to them.'[3]

The date that settled farming of a sort entered Britain is being set further and further back by radio-carbon dating, now probably into the fourth millennium BC. The evolving of comfortable homes suitable to our climate would have more than one and a half millennia to develop from such a date to the heyday of Stonehenge Britain; and this in the explosion of human thought and activity that came with the discovery of metals. Stonehenge society must have had homes – they have not been detected.

The significance of a change of interpretative emphasis away from ritual towards everyday living may be seen from this quotation in *Field Archaeology*, published by the Ordnance Survey in 1963. It says, 'The great company of round barrows implying population and the frequent finds of pottery, bronze weapons and tools of high quality belonging to the Bronze Age suggest that Bronze Age dwellings should be often found. So far they have been very elusive. A search through the records will show many signs of local settled life of a kind, but never in association with anything much more impressive than open hearths and rubbish pits. . . . The houses are not absent for the lack of wood-working tools and the skill with which to build them. Those who made the timber causeways belonging to this period which have been found in the Somerset Fens and East Anglia did not live in the open air.

'In Wessex the relative brilliance of the culture of those responsible for the final constructional phase of Stonehenge is shown by the rich contents of their graves, but we have no real idea of precisely where and how they lived.'[4]

Writing in the same year, 1963, the Ordnance Survey stated a major archaeological problem, and Mr Humphrey Case put forward a suggestion that could lead towards its solution, for there are structurally related monuments to the ring-ditches at Stanton

Harcourt in large numbers over many parts of southern Britain, in the form of other ring-ditches, saucer-barrows, disc-barrows, and henges.

Archaeologists dealing in prehistory face special difficulties, not present in the problems of mediaeval or Roman archaeologists, who have derived a working knowledge of their period from documentary sources. The social life of a manor or villa is known in outline and archaeology is only a supplement providing further detailed knowledge to fill this in. In prehistory, the situation is different. The archaeologist must attempt to reconstruct the entire social picture from the remains of man. Here lies the particular difficulty of the Bronze Age in Britain. Without the discovery of any homes of the ordinary men, not to mention the chieftains, how can social life be reconstructed? It is this fact more than any other that accounts for Stonehenge being just a fascinating enigma, a question-mark, rather than a monument that falls understandably into the sequence of our history. Without the home of Stonehenge man, his everyday life is a closed book to us, and we grope blindly for any sort of picture of his social organisation.

If we did have his home we could see whether he lived in small or large groups; whether its type was differentiated for chieftain and tribesman, or egalitarian; whether it revealed a design for times of peace or war; whether the great buildings of the Stonehenge area, and others, were built by a large local population for its everyday enjoyment, or to be visited as perhaps lonely buildings in a sacred area.

If Beaker man lived in the rudimentary ring-ditches in the Thames valley, what did he live in elsewhere where his remains are more evident – at say Lambourn Seven Barrows and Stonehenge? Here, at Stanton Harcourt is a *structure* that Stonehenge man may have built to live in – a circular ditched enclosure. What could resemble this at the greater known centres of population?

Virtually all structures of Stonehenge time are circular and fall into two categories: (1) henges, generally thought of as temple or ritual sites, (2) round barrows, seemingly built for the interment of the dead. In general, this exhausts all known types of Late Neolithic and Early Bronze Age structures (other than cursuses, which are outside this discussion) and, it is fair to say, their commonly ascribed purpose – ritual and burial of the dead. Elsewhere then, at the great centres of population such as Stonehenge, there are two types of structure resembling ring-ditches if for the sole reason that they take the same simple form – a circle.

To account for the absence of houses, it has often been suggested or maintained that Stonehenge man was a pastoralist, moving about with his herds and flocks, and living in temporary structures such as tents or perhaps light wattle huts that have left no trace. This lack of trace would be the more accountable as it is known that the chalk downs have eroded down $1\frac{1}{2}$ to 2 feet in the last three or four thousand years and the remains of any but deep post-holes would have disappeared. The erection of large public buildings such as Stonehenge and Woodhenge could be explained by the convening of pastoral peoples from a large area to execute the work. On their completion these would disperse, only to congregate again at festival times.

The possibility of human habitation in ring-ditches at Stanton Harcourt makes one look again at all ringed structures of the period, and leads to the posing of these alternatives: either (1) Stonehenge man led a pastoral or nomadic tribal existence living in tents or other temporary homes that have left no trace, an obsession with religion being expressed in numerous temples and elaborate burials for his dead; or (2) Stonehenge man led a static, tribal existence in permanent homes, and some of the seeming temples and burial places were in fact these homes. The wandering Fenian bands and the static tribes coexisted at the same time in Ireland, and no doubt different types of societies were present in the earlier time of Stonehenge Britain according to varying questions of geography and economy; but basically the question of the mode of life of Stonehenge man resolves itself between the alternatives above.

In essence the problem is one of assessing the purpose for which Stonehenge man enclosed numerous areas with a circular bank and ditch. The most impressive of these circular monuments are the henges, with a bank outside the ditch, and one or more entrances. Partially allied to these in structure are the disc-barrows, which are circular and have their bank outside the ditch, but which differ in not usually having an entrance. It is probable that the resemblance between the structure of henges and disc-barrows shows some link, however general, between the two in the mind of Stonehenge man, and it may be that this circular design is reflected in nearly all structures of the period for whatever purpose they were intended. Just as a modern builder first sets out his corners, so a Stonehenge builder first marked his circle with central stake and rotating length of cord. There can be no certainty that all henges and all disc-barrows were constructed with exactly the same purpose in mind in each case. It is possible that house, temple and burial place could reflect each other in some aspects.

In general, henges have been thought to be temples for two reasons. The first is that their bank is outside their ditch, which has seemed to indicate a non-military design. It can be appreciated that if one constructs a purely earthwork defence, the ditch is dug *outside* the bank, as in the later Iron Age hill-forts, and by this means an attacker is placed at a disadvantage as he drops into the ditch below the defender, on or behind the bank above. The second reason favouring the temple theory is that few henge monuments have revealed on excavation profuse debris of human occupation. Many finds have been made, but not the quantities of animal bones that might be expected from the remains of meals, and in general no great quantity of broken pottery.

The belief that henges are temples has had the overwhelming weight of opinion behind it since speculation regarding their purpose first began, and this view would not be lightly discarded. But one recalls again that practical and experienced archaeologist, Mr Paul Ashbee, writing in doubt, 'Henges and related structures have long been claimed as temples, but it is a strange society that constructs imposing groups of temples and no houses'.

There is a presupposition of the purpose of disc-barrows from the fact that they frequently contain one or more burials. Their association in groups with mounds that also commonly contain burials, has led to their primary purpose not being seriously questioned as burial structures for the dead, if one excepts Mr Case's question regarding the related structures, ring-ditches, and Professor Childe's comment.

This outlines what has been the accepted view on Late Neolithic and Bronze Age structures, and it leaves untouched the problem of habitation stated by the Ordnance Survey '. . . we have no real idea of where and how they lived'.

Now let us look at the case for the alternative, namely, that Stonehenge man lived in some of these structures. One recent development makes this possibility considerably less unlikely. That is the excavation at Clickhimin, which revealed an architectural design adapted to a circular plan, and made feasible a hitherto unthought of method of building construction in circles of unlimited diameter.

A single building in most circles – even the smaller disc-barrows of say ninety feet across – has not been considered because of the impossibility of barbarian man spanning such a distance with a roof. Clickhimin has at least given us an architectural concept that sweeps aside this difficulty.

It will be remembered that the fort at Clickhimin had peripheral buildings with an open courtyard in the centre. There is one building in the time of Stonehenge that has a basically similar design, namely, Woodhenge, and before the Clickhimin report Professor Stuart Piggott had already suggested that this was a circular building with a central open courtyard. Mr Hamilton suspects that forts – wooden but otherwise similar to the Scottish Clickhimin – existed in southern Britain at such places as West Harling in Norfolk, and the pattern of post-holes at these sites closely resembles that at Woodhenge. (The pattern is strikingly similar at the Iron Age house at Pimperne, Dorset, and the excavators of the house at West Harling discuss its reconstruction in the light of Woodhenge.) But West Harling is a site of the later Iron Age. The discrepancy between Clickhimin and Woodhenge need not then lie in architecture or in geography but in date – a gap of one and a half thousand years.

Is it conceivable that this gap can be bridged? A parallel from Irish archaeology makes a bridging at least conceivable. In that country is a type of structure known as a 'ring-fort'. There are known to be more than thirty thousand of these distributed all over Ireland. Some ring-forts are defined now by a stone rampart or vestigial standing stones, and others by a bank and ditch. The great number of ring-forts in Ireland shows that this was the usual dwelling at one time. The archaeological term 'ring-fort' must cover structures that varied considerably in architectural detail over a long period of time, but at least these structures must have embodied the functions of habitation and defence.

Their shape is most frequently circular as the name suggests, and the bank is sometimes outside the ditch, resembling a disc-barrow in Britain when this occurs. The proven range of time that this 'ring-fort' type of structure was in use in Ireland is from the Early Bronze Age to the seventeenth century AD – a span of over three thousand years. This lessens any innate unlikelihood that a basic architectural design for habitation could have persisted in Britain from the time of Woodhenge to that of West Harling.

To continue with the characteristics of these Irish ring-forts: excavation has revealed clearly that they were inhabited from the occupation material present, yet some have contained burials. At Cush, Co. Limerick, for instance, there were burials contained in Bronze Age urns. So one has both habitation and burial in the same buildings, and it can safely be presumed that the buildings in these cases were not erected primarily to house the dead but the living.

Irish ring-forts were often built touching each other, conjoined to form groups. This pattern was repeated at the ring-ditch complex at Stanton Harcourt, and is a common feature with disc-barrows in general in Britain. Teach Cormaic, one of the ring-forts at Tara, has a striking resemblance to a circular structure on Silk Hill, three miles north-east of Woodhenge. The sepulchral purpose of the Silk Hill monument (Milston no. 12) could be implied from its being in a Wessex Culture collection of barrows; yet no burial was found in it on extensive excavation by Colt Hoare. Apart from this monument and Teach Cormac having similar raised central platforms and having an approximately similar ditch, bank, ditch, sequence around them, coincidence is carried further by both structures having a diminutive barrow conjoined to them. Superficially, the Bronze Age circular structures of Britain and the Irish habitational ring-forts have a great deal in common.

Let us go back to Woodhenge. In support of a conception of it as a temple, it has been claimed that there was little debris of human life found at it on excavation. The evidence is this: the Cunningtons showed that there were 156 post-holes arranged in its interior. Of these, 130 post-holes contained remains of animals – bone, teeth, horn, antler – and 85 contained pottery, worked or burnt flint. Six pits were found just outside the ditch and each of these contained amongst other debris 'many animal bones'.

The evidence suggested to Mrs Cunnington that the site of Woodhenge had been cultivated since Romano-British times, and one can observe that any concentration of debris would consequently have tended to disperse over a wide area. Most of the bank had been destroyed by cultivation, which in recent times alone had gone on for seventy or eighty years, but even so Mrs Cunnington writes, 'Wherever there were remains of the bank relics were found in the old surface layer beneath it, consisting mostly of broken animal bones and scattered fragments of pottery'.[5] Considerable quantities of pottery were found in the ditch. (A similar distribution of pottery finds was revealed at the Iron Age house at West Harling—in the post-holes and ditch.)

Woodhenge is then very far from being the 'clean site' that would be expected from a place solely used for ritual; except for this point – ancient ritual, in Homer's world for instance, usually entailed feasting, with resulting animal bones and broken pottery. Is the evidence at Woodhenge that of everyday eating and living, or that of occasional feasting?

Mr Case makes a very important point regarding the Stanton Harcourt ring-ditches, which could be relevant to Woodhenge. He says that if the ring-ditches are ritual sites, there should be settlement sites in the area. But after watching the commercial gravel diggers of the Oxford district for thirty years no such settlement sites have been revealed. No equivalent commercial excavation over wide areas has gone on on the downs, but after some centuries of observation and excavation it is surely strange that no settlement sites have been found. The animal bones and pottery at Woodhenge and other ringed structures may not be profuse, but there is evidence of virtually none anywhere else.

It is a frustrating fact that known settlement sites of various periods in the Highland Zone of Britain are frequently almost devoid of datable material. Woodhenge has far more to show than this. One can be sure that many domestic utensils would have been made of wood and skins, which would be unlikely to survive, and the making of pottery may not have been as common as might be supposed.

Let us pretend to commit ourselves and assume that Woodhenge was a two-storeyed dwelling, in its possible twenty or thirty feet of height, after the type of Clickhimin, and that it was inhabited by a royal, tribal household similar to that of Tara revealed in Irish epic. Wild as this pretence may seem, it is only carrying further a picture of considerable power, talent and organisation that has been becoming clearer in recent years but in fields other than habitation and architecture. If Woodhenge was a royal fort, after the Tara tradition (and the earthworks at Tara are not dissimilar), everyday life would take place mainly on the first floor, and much of the debris of living would fall here in the first instance. The caste system of Irish society is shown in their myths, and the rooms would be cleaned to some reasonable barbarian standard by members of a lower caste. Here would be a reason for the six pits with 'many animal bones' at Woodhenge, and also reason to suspect other rubbish dumps elsewhere, where the bulk of the rubbish of Woodhenge might be found, rather than in its interior. Other pits with animal bones and debris in fact have been found near Woodhenge, and have been an instance of the archaeological interpretation of 'ritual pits'. However visualised, the ultimate resting place of rubbish falling on a wooden first-storey floor is likely to be different from that falling to and being trodden into the ground.

Let us turn now to the question of burials in ringed structures. The term 'barrow' implies a burial mound, and 'disc-barrow' similarly a structure built for the dead. And yet, many disc-barrows on excavation are found to contain no burial. The dissolving of the bones by an acid soil only accounts for this in some regions away from the downs as these latter are alkaline. Assuming that the primary purpose of disc-barrows was not for burial, what would account for the presence of burials in many of them?

It has already been mentioned that Woodhenge has a central burial of a child, whose skull had been intentionally cleft completely into two halves. There has been general acceptance that this can be little other than a dedication sacrifice to Woodhenge itself, as a building. The burial's significant near-central position exactly on the axis of the monument makes this probable. So here is a reversal of an assumed purpose of disc-barrows, which were thought to have been built to house the dead, for at Woodhenge the sequence seems to have been that a building was required for another purpose and a sacrifice was incidentally placed in it for propitiatory reasons. The central or near-central position of the Woodhenge burial is similar to that in disc-barrows.

The practice of dedicatory burials in buildings has been a common one of mankind. In the Stonehenge period, there was the burial of two women, half under the wall and half under a bed of one of the houses at Skara Brae, and this of one of the cultures prominent at Woodhenge, the Rinyo-Clacton. In this case, there can be no doubt that ritual and burial were incidental to considerations of everyday life. The inference seems to be that magic was present but in a subsidiary role. There was a burial inside one of the ring-ditches at Stanton Harcourt which Mr Case suggests might be a habitation structure. The Bronze Age burials in the ring-fort at Cush, Co. Limerick, have already been mentioned. In the Iron Age, a fort in Scotland similar to Clickhimin had a central burial in it, although

Clickhimin itself did not. The Rath of the Synods at Tara had five central burials in it.

In view of the fact that some disc-barrows have no burials in them at all, and in other ringed or habitation structures such burials are only secondary to the main purpose of the structure, it is at least feasible that disc-barrows are not primarily burial structures at all. Is it in these and in some of the henges that Stonehenge man lived?

In nearly every case where the sex of the burial in disc-barrows has been determined, it has been female. This conclusion is strengthened by the feminine nature of the grave-goods associated, such as beads, etc. It may be a parallel fact that in Irish mythology all the royal centres are reputed to have a founder goddess buried at them, from whom their names are often taken, the goddess Macha at Emain Macha, for instance. These goddesses were looked on as founts for tribal fertility, and while there is no archaeological evidence of the specific location of these goddess burials in Irish palaces (although the central burial in the Clickhimin-type fort mentioned above could be relevant by being of the period), there is the possibility that the female burials in disc-barrows were placed similarly to promote the well-being of its inhabitants. The burials in the house at Skara Brae were female and the sex of the child at Woodhenge was probably female according to the report. Again, the benefit of the sympathetic magical effect of a warrior burial to a structure in time of war is consistent with primitive belief.

The long-used word 'earthwork' may soon have served its term in British archaeology. There is implicit in the word that prehistoric man embarked on making a structure, a 'work', made solely of earth. On the other hand, the vestiges of the buildings of historic man are not called earthworks, because the structures they commemorate can be visualised. The houses of a deserted mediaeval village rise in the mind's eye from the turfed banks that are all that is left on the surface. The imagination legitimately supplies the great timber rampart and tower of an early Norman castle on a motte, which was merely the earthen plinth to a functional and intricate structure. In centuries to come, a present-day farmer's field bank and ditch will seem a feeble, valueless 'earthwork' without the perishable posts and strands of barbed wire above it. We are at the commencement of a period of archaeological interpretation in which most prehistoric banks, ditches and mounds will be seen similarly as vestiges of intricate structures with many varying functions. It is

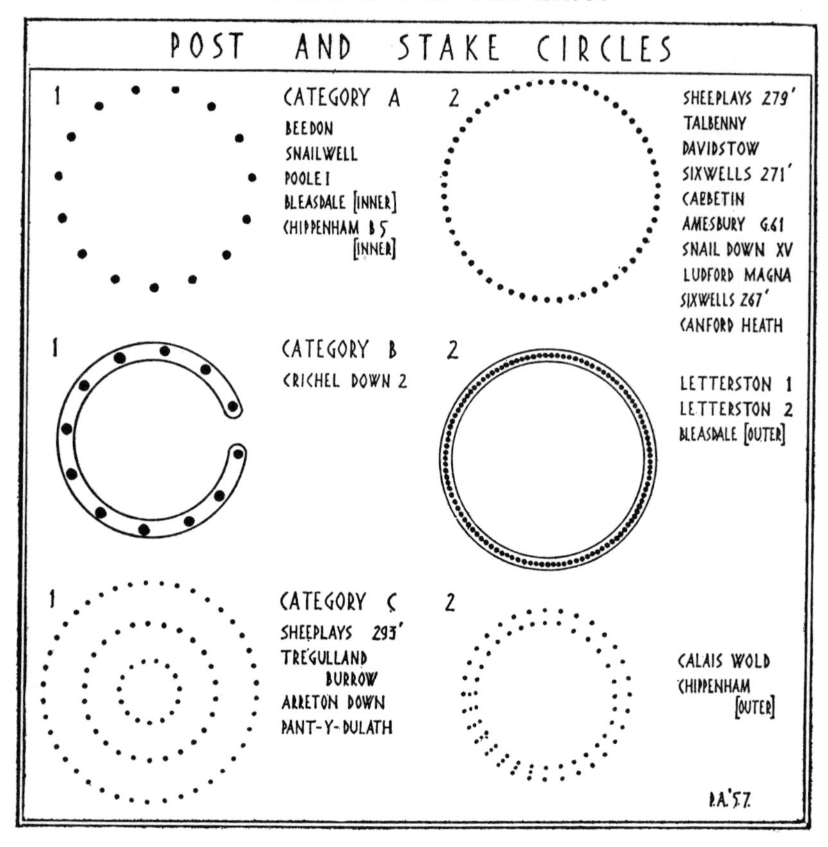

Fig. E. Patterns of post and stake circles under barrows. Note Crichel Down, with posts in ditch showing causeway. A barrow in this group was noted as having occupation soil with Beaker pottery, one of an increasing number revealing occupation evidence.

Fig. F. (*opposite*) Plan of the Sanctuary (*top*) of the second millenium BC. The three settings of post-holes shown separately are in fact superimposed. Plans of habitation structures of first millenium BC (*bottom*); (1) Little Woodbury, Wilts. (2) Kester, Devon (3) Scotstarvit, Fife (4) West Plean, Stirlingshire. Note again the tendency in both second and first millenium buildings to have outer small posts, close-set, and inner, large, spaced posts.

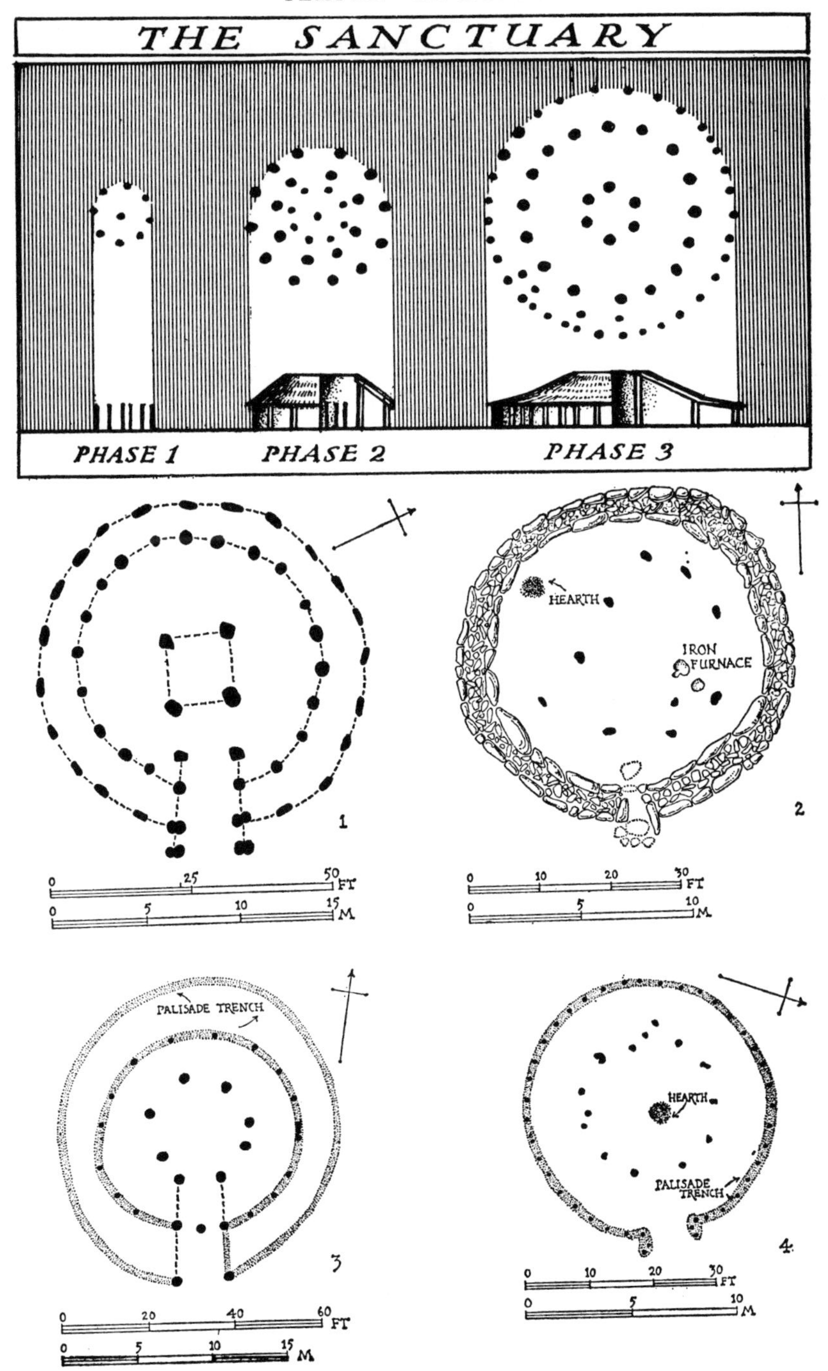
THE SANCTUARY
PHASE 1
PHASE 2
PHASE 3
HEARTH
IRON FURNACE
1
2
0 25 50 FT
0 5 10 15 M
0 10 20 30 FT
0 5 10 M
PALISADE TRENCH
HEARTH
PALISADE TRENCH
3
4
0 20 40 60 FT
0 5 10 15 M
0 10 20 30 FT
0 5 10 M

now known that the weathered domes of some round barrows give no hint of their original shape, which must have been drum-like within a circular retaining structure. Many barrows – in Holland as well as Britain – have revealed a pattern of post- and stake-holes beneath them, and while the purpose of such settings is not yet clear, these show that the barrow was far more than a simple, thrown-up mound of earth when it was constructed. Many barrow-like structures, other than the Stanton Harcourt ring-ditches, have contained occupation material, and it must be borne in mind that raised platform-type ring-forts exist in Ireland, which might parallel in some instances the raised mounds invariably assigned as barrows (although not uncommonly without burials) in Britain. If the excavation reports are read through it is found that considerable numbers of barrow-like structures did have entrance causeways; some of the Crichel Down group in Dorset are so provided, and so are a number of the ring-ditches in the Oxford area, for example. The causeways, indicators of a purpose of repeated transit, could be for continuing ritual at the monuments, but perhaps the burden of proof is thrown most heavily on advocates of the ritualistic theory. Nevertheless, great bowl-barrows, such as Bush and Clandon Barrows with their regalia, suggest purely sepulchral structures.

The changing processes of thought regarding Woodhenge set a pattern, as it were, for future reinterpretations of many 'earthworks'. Before Squadron-Leader Insall's aerial observation, Woodhenge was thought to be a disc-barrow – an earthbound structure. After the Cunningtons' excavation, it soared upward into an open temple of wooden posts to an unknown, primitive religion. With Professor Piggott's interpretation it can now be seen as a potentially functional building with, one could comment, every possibility in its design of strong defence and comfortable communal living. The concept of people of limited ambition and ability laboriously digging a functionless 'earthwork' has been left far behind in this case. It may be that the evidence of timber structure has remained so clearly at Woodhenge because of the great size and depth of its post-holes, thereby escaping obliteration by erosion, but many other structures of the same period have resemblances to Woodhenge. The henge at Arminghall in Norfolk with its large post-holes springs to mind, as does the Sanctuary in the Avebury complex.

These evidences of complex structure in what had been thought of as simple earthen features will lead archaeological thought on to many reassessments. For instance, it has been an axiom of archaeology in Britain that when an enclosure has its bank outside its ditch, the structure must be a ritual one. It is true that such an enclosure is useless for defence, *if it was built solely of earth.* If, on the other hand, there was a timber or stone wall on the inner side of the ditch – as at Woodhenge – there is nowhere to place the spoil from the ditch other than on the outside. The large enclosure around the remains of Emain Macha in Ireland is defined as a hill-fort, and yet it has its bank outside its ditch. Nowhere in Ireland has more annals of war attaching to it than Emain Macha, and one can be virtually certain – without the archaeological evidence – that this ditch had an inner wall behind it. Archaeologists, writing in quite recent years, do not raise such a possibility and are merely puzzled by such an apparently defenceless structure at a known site of war. Ritual purposes have even been suggested here at Cu Chulainn's stronghold.

The process could be reversed by visualising the fine stone-fort in Ireland, Staigue Fort, Kerry, robbed of its circular stone rampart standing twenty feet high or more, as it possibly would have been in a less remote area. All that would be left would be its encircling ditch and outer bank, an apparent defenceless earthwork, of puzzling function because of its slight nature. It may be that in time to come an archaeologist's first thought in excavating a structure with a bank outside a ditch will be to seek the evidence of an inner wall – perhaps in fact eroded away, or not present because a sleeper-beam or merely resting timber construction was used as in some early buildings in Ireland – rather than to seek the evidence of ritual. Weather erosion must have obliterated many post-holes in lesser buildings than Woodhenge.

Until most recently there was no cause to contemplate these architectural possibilities, but Clickhimin has forced them upon us. We now know that prehistoric man in Britain was living in comfort in his first- and second-storey rooms, and this in the backward and conservative extreme north. Our vision of him must be raised above the humble 'earthworks' that are the ruins of his period in the south. These smooth outlined 'earthworks' on the downs' surface, fallen by 1½ feet, are merely the faint reminders of structures.

There is a puzzling type of structure known as a 'Highworth Circle'. About forty of these are located around Highworth in north-east Wiltshire. In shape they resemble a disc-barrow, but with no central tump, and they are of large diameter, sometimes over a hundred yards. They are situated on clay, and on occasion when I have visited them some of their ditches have been filled with water. In spite of their resemblance to disc-barrows, their situation on clay is most unusual for a Bronze Age structure, and the possibility that they are not of the Bronze Age is increased by the fact that Romano-British pottery has been found on excavation 2–3 feet deep in one of their ditches. If these Highworth Circles were in fact Romano-British there is no parallel religious group of structures in this period to suggest that they were in any way ritual, and it might be suspected that they were used for habitation. The absence of an entrance causeway across the ditch in these circles and in disc-barrows merely presupposes the former existence of a perishable wooden bridge. It will be remembered that the span of use of ring-forts in Ireland was three thousand years. The possibility arises that not only might variations of Clickhimin architecture span back to Woodhenge, but that it might exceptionally span forward to Romano-British times, a duration of over two thousand years.

It is probable that in the past we have regarded late prehistoric man as too transient in his stay at settlement sites. Returning to Stanton Harcourt in Oxfordshire, the complex of Late Neolithic ring-ditches is closely set in the remains of a settlement of Iron Age times. Not only are Iron Age huts, enclosures and boundaries clustered around the Late Neolithic complex, but storage or rubbish pits of the two periods are mingled together also. Case, from his long experience of this area, comments that this mingling is a 'typical situation regionally'.[6] The structural evidence of such a span of continued occupation occurs at many places elsewhere, such as Maiden Castle, the Trundle in Sussex, and at Rams Hill in Berkshire it continues into Romano-British times. Both the Late Neolithic and Iron Age pits at Stanton Harcourt contained the bones of ox, pig, goat and sheep. The pottery present in and around the complex ranged through Peterborough (Late Neolithic), Beaker, Middle Bronze Age, Iron Age, Romano-Belgic and Romano-British, that is, from pre-2000 BC right into our own era.

Mr Case himself draws a conclusion that the ring-ditches at Stanton Harcourt, similar as they are in design to disc-barrows, were used from Peterborough times to the Middle or possibly Late Bronze Age. This is quite at variance with the interpretation of the limited period usually assigned to disc-barrows in the Wessex Culture period only. The question arises as to the whole period of actual use of many monuments. There is a tendency once one has arrived at the initial period of building of a monument to assign little or no significance to pottery found at it of a considerably later period. At Stonehenge and Arminghall, for instance, Iron Age and Romano-British pottery was present and Woodhenge revealed Romano-British. Once these great structures were built it is unlikely that they were not kept in repair and used for a period of centuries, bridging the time and cultures from the Late Neolithic towards the Iron Age. Mediaeval timber-framed buildings survive today. The North Ferriby ships show a potential of superb construction and maintenance.

Not only does the long span of use of the Stanton Harcourt ring-ditch complex from the Late Neolithic to the Middle or Late Bronze Age argue for settlement rather than ceremonial, but it suggests that perhaps the detailed analysis of pottery resulting in its very specific association with varied ringed structures of limited periods has masked the simple fact that ringed structures were in use for two thousand years or more in Britain. If one of the uses is accepted as that of habitation, it means that there was a common thread running through the organisation of society from Late Neolithic to Iron Age times and beyond, and that the society preceding the Late Bronze Age was not fundamentally different from that following, as had been thought.

The clumping of Wessex Culture barrows by the earlier henges and cursuses is marked. The clumped areas of ruins, such as at Stonehenge and Oakley-Knowlton, must be significant. Individual monuments in these concentrations were built at different times from the Neolithic to the Bronze Age, but the settled life of each community ran through this time, using its buildings as Londoners use Westminster Abbey, Buckingham Palace, and the Festival Hall, built in their different periods, today. I think we have in these areas of ruins a historic map of Wessex, showing the royal capitals; showing in themselves social organisation and the ruins of the population of more than a thousand years of our history. I have used the word 'cities' earlier in the book to implant their unity. The collective idea of palace households, clustered clan homes, public buildings and processional ways, and the ancestral roots of power must be expressed to describe each area of ruins.

The similar regalias near Stonehenge in Bush Barrow and in Clandon Barrow by Dorchester demand the concept of kingship and kingdoms. I equate this concept with the ruins at Lambourn, Avebury, Stonehenge, Oakley-Knowlton and Dorchester. I think each is the capital of a kingdom – a royal capital. The concentrated areas of ruins are in a sense the kingdoms themselves in that the population of each domain was concentrated in them. The large areas of relatively unpopulated territory surrounding each represents jealously guarded terrain, ripe for cattle-raiding, but also an evolved insulation between one warrior society and the next, as in ancient Greece.

And so we come back to Clickhimin, probably the most illuminating excavation ever carried out on a structure of barbarian northern Europe.

I accept the implications of Clickhimin: that the architectural link between it and buildings suggested and potentially visualised at Tara and Woodhenge is too strong to be broken. Inevitably accompanying this acceptance must come a recognisable concept of Stonehenge society; a concept which is new and unexpected, and yet which falls naturally and understandably into its context in European history as a whole.

Ancient Ireland was divided into five provinces or kingdoms, with the high-king holding a traditional suzerainty over the whole land at Tara. The provincial capitals were generally unchanging seats of power immemorially revered, such as Cruachan and Emain Macha. The beginnings of such kingdoms in England may appear in the ruins of the Wessex Culture at sites already traditionally revered in Cornwall, Norfolk, Knowlton, Poor Lot, Lambourn Seven Barrows and Derbyshire. Given such a political concept, the seat of supreme power in Wessex at least can be nowhere other than the Stonehenge capital.

I conceive Woodhenge to be the British counterpart of Tara, architecturally, socially and historically; the palace-fort of the High-king. I see it set in the Stonehenge capital with the round palaces and houses of petty chiefs and aristocrats of the king's court and their households rising stark and grouped around the great focal buildings and interspersed with the tombs of their ancestors.

We know so much of Tara. We could now be set on the way to understand nearly as much of Stonehenge Britain.

REFERENCES

1. Case, Humphrey, 'Notes on Finds and Ring-ditches in the Oxford Region', *Oxoniensia*, XXVIII, 1963.

2. Case, Humphrey, *op. cit.*

3. Grinsell, L. V., *The Archaeology of Wessex*, Methuen, 1958.

4. Ordnance Survey, *Field Archaeology*, Her Majesty's Stationery Office, 1963.

5. Cunnington, M. E., *Woodhenge*, 1929.

6. Case, Humphrey, *op. cit.*

CHAPTER 17

The New Concept

THERE IS a school of archaeological thought which regards Late Neolithic and Bronze Age society as not having been essentially warlike, the battle-axes and daggers being interpreted as prestige possessions, and all henges being regarded as defenceless places of ritual. Such a society would have had to exist in a Britain that was an oasis of peace in Europe with Mycenae expending its greatest energy on building its Citadel at one extreme and Ireland concentrating on ring-forts at the other. It would be linked by the archaeological evidence of its weapons and trade to heroic societies such as Mycenae, Brittany and central Europe and yet be not of them. Almost its entire communal energy would be expended on temple building and ritual in a Europe that all the evidence suggests thrived on battle. To me, this anomaly is too great to accept.

Professor Stuart Piggott wrote in 1965 that '... the world of second millennium barbarian Europe was essentially the world of the *Iliad* ...' The *Iliad* is man's archetypal story of war. And again he writes, 'The arms race had been on from at least the fourth millennium BC in the Ancient Orient and there is no sign that the European barbarians showed any reluctance in learning the new arts of war made possible by improved weapons. More and more the archaeological evidence begins to reflect the existence, over most of Europe, of a warrior aristocracy of a type familiar to us from heroic and epic literature ranging from the *Iliad* to the *Sagas*; from the *Rig-Veda* to the *Tain Bo Cuailnge* (*The Cattle Raid of Cooley*, P.C.).'[1] These have one basic tale to tell – that of war.

The *Iliad* undoubtedly reflects some aspects of Mycenaean society. It is notable that the Greek army has no priests accompanying it. There are seers but these are merely warriors with special powers; the heroes conduct their own sacrificial rites. The situation is similar with Jason's crew. The Greek warrior had created his gods of war and he needed little outside help in dealing with them. His magic surrounded his leader in war – the king. Archaeological research has revealed no large temples in the Mycenaean world. The kings and warriors of the *Iliad* are too concerned with the priorities of living and killing to be unduly worried by the mysticism of religion. M. I. Finley writes in *The World of Odysseus*, '. . . there was no reverential fear of the gods . . . For moral support the men of the Iliad relied not on the gods but on their fellow-men . . .'.[2]

The fickle gods of the Mycenaean Greeks were little more than Moira, fate. They take sides indiscriminately and the heroes are not daunted by their presence on the battlefield. There is no moral sense or ecstasy of devotion; the religious fanaticism of Cromwell's Roundheads is not for the early Greeks. Magic is everywhere but is subsidiary to the joy of combat, and, other than the sacrifice, religion is largely uncodified and non-ritual.

As with the Mycenaean warrior, so with the Celtic. For the Celtic hero, pleasure, war and life were indivisible; religion was outside and beneath this. He sometimes fought naked, vaingloryingin strife. The gods were an adjunct in the pursuit of war. The druids read omens, philosophise and teach; but the presiding magic figure at the festivals is the king, who brings tribal victory. The independent Celt built no temples; his efforts were expended on buildings he was compelled to have for war. So again with the Norse warriors, who were promised a continuance of their greatest pleasures, fighting and feasting, by Odin in Valhalla.

These are the oldest surviving European traditions stemming from a common Indo-European origin and they tell of little but war. Thoughts of magic filled all men's minds, but it would be unwise to over-stress the likelihood of this producing a united surge of extreme fervour in worship of a god or gods. Mr T. G. E. Powell says in *The Celts*, 'To seek for a clear-cut body of belief, in the sense of the great historical religions, to expect consistency or conformity of views about life after death, or of the relation of man to the supernatural, whether gods or beings less defined, would be to mistake the whole nature of trans-Alpine barbarism in Pre-Roman times.'[3]

There is a basic simplicity in the earlier Mother Goddess involved in supplying desperately needed necessities for man to survive; but the gods of High Barbarian Europe were onlookers as man played at his sport of war – onlookers from mountain tops and forest glades, for there is no tradition in Europe of there being temples built for them in which to live. Men were too busy, living and fighting.

Man is the great predator; predatory as much to his own species as to others. Wars are not isolated catastrophes in the history of man, but one of the major themes in his history. To look back for a Golden Age of temple building at the time in Britain when man first had efficient weapons in his hands is the negation of history. Many circular earthworks in Britain must be the remains of his defence structures.

It would be wrong to advance this thesis as a declamation – 'Stonehenge Britain Solved!' The interpretation of prehistory allows no easy solution, and a number of archaeologists have the thoughts I have written down much in their minds. No modern archaeologist has advanced a firm view on the organisation of Stonehenge society, but the emphasis on ritual and religion in all writings to the present gives a continuous theme of similar interpretation back through Victorian times for two hundred years or more. The evidence from most archaeological sites is not without ambiguity, and some archaeologists will say that the evidence from circular structures of Late Neolithic and Bronze Age Britain is not strong enough to support the interpretation of defensive tribal homes. Against this, what is there now to support their interpretation as temples? Perhaps little more than a dead weight of interpretation from the past. This is not quite true, but I have said it to bring out that one cannot say when faced with this question, on the one hand, 'These buildings are temples', and then if pressed, on the other, blandly, 'We simply do not know.' The evidence now is such in my opinion that the problem should be re-approached with an open mind.

Having advanced the thesis of tribal-forts in Stonehenge Britain for the first time, my own view is naturally committed. I think that if Stonehenge Britain is viewed in this light, the weapons with the burials, the architectural evidence, and the earliest documentary material of Europe all blend into a suddenly unfolding comprehensible whole, instead of the anomalous entities they have appeared before. For this view to achieve universal acceptance – which I think it will in time – there is no great need for specific excavation directed towards its proving or disproving. Britain is one of the more archaeologically active nations, and innumerable reports exist of excavations of circular structures that present all the types of evidence that will possibly ever be available, although more positive architectural evidence could come to light at any time, as it did in unlooked for form at Clickhimin. Modern excavation seeks to report all evidence whether appearing of interest or not from a site. The catalyst to all the existing evidence is Mr Hamilton's excavation at Clickhimin. If one wishes to assess the evidence in the light of this, one can 'excavate' into past reports from Britain and Ireland, and seek an interpretative balance. I have done this, and the result is too detailed to advance in a book of this nature, but in my view, while it would be foolish to consider that all the circular structures of Stonehenge Britain fall into one category or are at a stroke completely comprehensible, enough is seen to give rebirth to a Stonehenge Britain living in tribal forts, with Woodhenge, Arminghall and the Sanctuary as prototypes. If this is true, and I think time will lead to its general acceptance, I consider that the illumination shed by Hamilton's excavation on barbarian Europe will be no less than that Schliemann shed on early Greece – understanding of the history of north-west Europe will be extended back for two thousand years. A historical discovery difficult to over-assess in its importance will have been made at the prehistoric fort at Clickhimin.

We have never had a social background against which to interpret Stonehenge Britain. Each little mite of archaeological fact won has been stuck on to an amorphous whole, with little increase of understanding. The essence of the people still lies utterly remote. I suspect that many will view such a new thesis, with its broad revealing sweep over northern Europe, as heretical. We have become conditioned to the laborious collection of minute fact with little increased meaning for decades. There will seem a lack of austere discipline in having a concept of Bronze Age Britain where each new fact is full of meaning and increases our understanding of the way its people lived.

The greatest re-orientation will be needed in the way we view the importance of the gods of prehistory. I believe that in an extraordinarily subtle way the dead hand of Victorian romanticism had continued to lead our thoughts almost exclusively down the paths of religion, diverting attention from the everyday life of the people.

It seems safe to presume that the pantheon of Stonehenge Britain will never be known. It is not necessary to our understanding that it should. There is enough parallel evidence when Stonehenge Britain is seen as a normal heroic society for us to know its type, revealed in Greece and Ireland. Comprehension comes with a concept of local, tribal, war and fertility gods, perhaps lightly overspread by deities similar to Lug and Boand. The Megalith Builders may have brought belief in such a deity in their spread past Mount Prescelly in the west. The key to Stonehenge thought is not priest-led obsession with an all-powerful deity, but the exigencies of everyday life, conditioned by traditional magic and the magic of the moment, which is channelled through the intermediary to the tribal gods, the king. A projection of similar gods can accompany that of not dissimilar heroic society back to 2000 BC.

In this book, I have frequently used the word 'trade' when writing of luxury goods found in exotic situations. For instance, the finding of a bronze dagger in a grave in Wessex – a non-metalliferous area – is usually accepted as evidence of trade (although there has been reasoning otherwise).

After Clickhimin, I do not agree with this conception. Trade to us means dealing in commodities for profit by barter or currency. Since the finding of so many exotic objects in Stonehenge Britain, we have commonly written of 'traders' (or sometimes 'merchant-adventurers'), 'trade routes', 'commercial networks', 'successful business men', and the like. The term 'merchant-adventurer' is half intrusive in this list, implying the gaining of wealth partly by means other than trade.

We agree that the remains of the Stonehenge people show evidence of royalty and aristocracy and that their society was probably 'heroic', a warrior society resembling that of Homeric Greece. Perhaps we have not fully accepted the implications of this: Odysseus never traded – he was a 'sacker of cities'.

One does not have to accept evidence limited to Homer's poetry. To a considerable extent, the wealth of warrior societies was linked to their military power. Allied to military power – the procuring of loot – was prestige and the power of advantageous alliance and overlordship. In the documents of ancient Greece and Ireland this was fostered by lavish hospitality and the exchange of luxury gifts – gifts so valuable that an unspoken obligation was implied on their receiver.

The measure of the success of a heroic society was the quantity of its loot and tribute, the scale on which it could lavish hospitality on visiting aristocracy, and the quality of the gifts it could bestow without impoverishing itself. Success in these things led to an ascending spiral of wealth, with outside men of power being increasingly attracted into its orbit.

The 'assets' did not include 'trading good-will', but were relative military strength and the magnetism of all the appurtenances of barbarian power. In this sense, the seeming 'marts' of ancient Europe really lay in the war forays for loot and in the feasts and festivals when the results of looting were passed on as gifts to influence and ally. 'Trade' was in such things as freedom from attack, intimidation and invasion, protection, states determined by the decisions of leaders of heroic societies. I think that this predominantly was the 'trade' of the heroic societies of ancient Europe, rather than the passing of goods in measured quantity for goods. The currency was political intrigue and war.

The heroic societies of Europe appear as localised but quite large worlds to themselves. Much of the diffusion of material and ideas would be from society to neighbouring society, by way of war and royal hospitality with inter-dynastic marriages, rather than by individual exploration, and when this latter did occur it would be led by warrior-aristocracy under royal sponsorship with material gain in mind. The North Ferriby ships fit well in this conception. It is in this light that I see the extraordinary assemblage of wealth in Wessex – the bronze pins from central Europe, the daggers, the gold from Ireland, the fine pottery from Brittany, the amber and the faience.

I see Wessex as an area of wealth and power dominated by five heroic communities. I see five kingdoms ruled from nucleated capitals at Lambourn, Avebury, Stonehenge, Oakley-Knowlton, and Dorchester. I see these areas of ruins on the map as not only representing monuments but population. It may appear utterly fruitless from these monuments to hazard at the size of population, but I do so: Lambourn – 1,000; Avebury – 4,000; Stonehenge – 10,000; Oakley-Knowlton – 3,000; Dorchester – 4,000. I merely do this to reinforce a prediction that some estimate of the population living at these capitals will be known in ten years' time.

I see the populations of the tribal capitals living in drum-tower, timber forts, two or more storeys high, some of the henges and barrows being the surviving remains of these. I see these structures housing a hundred up to considerably greater numbers in each. In the absence of above-ground timber structure, it can only be imaginative to visualise specific design, but I think that the encircling ditch indicates a necessary feature for the drainage of a large, out-sloping roof (and the sanitation of a dense community), perhaps covered by shingles; that this roof came over a rampart walk, opening from upper storey rooms; that some structures (perhaps those of greater area) had an open courtyard in the centre for cattle, with some ground floor byres and also workshops; that other structures were purely palace households, with radial rooms between the fort wall and a central or off-central hall in which was the great hearth with a smoke-vent in the roof above. The standard of carpentry shown by the North Ferriby ships hints at the quality of their construction and long life.

I see these drum-towers clustered and scattered at the capitals; in some cases abutting on one another. Each capital would be the royal seat of a kingdom whose realm would stretch to a common border with its neighbouring kingdom, the River Stour, for instance, perhaps being the traditional frontier between Dorchester and Oakley-Knowlton.

I see the societies in these capitals being geared for war, the equivalent of the 'Leader of the Host' being responsible to the king for the constant manning of the gates and ramparts, and for the safe closing of the gates at night. A society of king, warrior-nobility (coupled with wise men), and free-commoner cattle-men would answer the requirements of war, with low-caste menials for the routine work. Smiths would be honoured according to reputation.

I see the kings and warrior class living in considerable barbarian luxury, in the comfort of upstairs rooms, with perhaps low table furniture (all the pottery is flat-based for smooth surfaces), to be sat at on palliasses, also used as beds. They would wear well tailored clothes, magnificently adorned, and would be shaved to the fashion of the day. I suggest that bathing was not necessarily unknown to them (the practice was widespread in heroic Europe).

War and feasting were not only the chief pursuits of the aristocracy but the mainspring of social economy. I think many of the remnants of structures that we see can be interpreted in the light of this, built for practical reasons and lived in by their builders. I conceive these societies speaking predominantly some early form of the Indo-European group of languages.

The scale of the ruins left at these capitals – largely undisturbed since their heyday – is the measure of their power in a world of heroic societies. The transcendance of the Stonehenge capital is obvious, and perhaps in Stonehenge itself we have the symbol of the general overlordship of many centuries. After Clickhimin, it must be apparent that people *lived in* the ruins at Tara as a royal seat. I think that Stonehenge is a misted reflection of Tara.

I think in correlating a concept of heroic Stonehenge society (long conditionally accepted), with Clickhimin architecture, and the five areas of ruins of Stonehenge Wessex, a general social frame emerges. This is new, but to my mind, it is understandable and has truth. Any interpretation of archaeological remains is subjective and speculative, but I think the seeds of truth lie in what I have written above. No doubt some of the rounding of the picture is facile. In the complete absence of direct social evidence of the Stonehenge world, one can only seek elsewhere for reflections. Human thought and action is strangely unpredictable and societies complex, but I think the framework of Stonehenge society lies in this rough pattern.

As I come towards the end of writing this book, I look back and realise that its mould is partly the development of my own thought. Perhaps as it stands, it is a more useful and interesting document, laying out a progress of thought and understanding in the course of its writing. The earlier part of the book is based on many long-held concepts, some of which may have to strive to maintain their place in Stonehenge Britain. The world goes on, and I believe that something true comes out at the end of the book, developed in the course of its writing. A momentous event occurred while it was being written – the revelation at Clickhimin. In a sense, my progress of thought paralleled the advance from Victorian understanding to the present day, and, if I may say so, breaking into the future. Since Victorian days, with its obsession with the religion of the ancients, we have had enormous increases in archaeological fact, but a microscopic increase in understanding. After Clickhimin, our understanding has suddenly caught up with our archaeology. Armed with this new knowledge, I foresee an unprecedented advance in our historical understanding in the immediate future.

Harold Macmillan predicted a wind of change blowing through Africa. How strong this wind proved to be! Clickhimin will blow a wind of change through the history of Britain and north-western

Europe. To those who are prepared to accept the implications of Clickhimin in the way I do, this wind has begun to blow. We sail on it into a suddenly unfolding world of Stonehenge Britain.

REFERENCES

1. Piggott, Stuart, *Ancient Europe*, Edinburgh University Press, 1965.
2. Finley, M. I., *The World of Odysseus*, Chatto and Windus, 1956.
3. Powell, T. G. E., *The Celts*, Thames and Hudson, 1958.

Select Bibliography

The works listed are supplementary to those acknowledged at chapter endings. Bersu is important for the overall roofing of some ring-forts (Lissue and Isle of Man); Ó Ríordáin (Ballycatteen Fort) for peripheral habitation in a large ring-fort; and O'Kelly (Carrigillihy) and Ó Ríordáin (Cush) for the early dating of ring-forts. Most of the works have been selected as having special bearing on barbarian architecture and social form over the British Isles as a whole.

Annable, F. K., and Simpson, D. D. A., *Guide Catalogue of the Neolithic and Bronze Age Collections in Devizes Museum*, 1963.

Ashbee, P., 'The Wilsford Shaft', *Antiquity*, XXXVII, 1963.

Bersu, G., 'Excavations at Little Woodbury, Wiltshire', *Proceedings of the Prehistoric Society*, VI, 1940.

Bersu, G., 'The Rath in Townland Lissue, Co. Antrim', *Ulster Journal of Archaeology*, X, 1947.

Bersu, G., 'Celtic Homesteads in the Isle of Man', *The Journal of the Manx Museum*, V, 1945.

Case, H., 'The Lambourn Seven Barrows', *Berkshire Archaeological Journal*, 55, 1956.

Clark, G., 'The Timber Monument at Arminghall and Its Affinities', *Proceedings of the Prehistoric Society*, II, 1936.

Clark, J. G. D., and Fell, C. T., 'The Early Iron Age Site at Micklemoor Hill, West Harling, Norfolk', *Proceedings of the Prehistoric Society*, XIX, 1953.

Crampton, P., *The Prehistoric Ridge Way: A Journey*, 1965.

Cross, T. P., and Slover, C. H., *Ancient Irish Tales*, 1936.

Cunnington, M. E., 'The Sanctuary on Overton Hill, near Avebury', *Wiltshire Archaeological Magazine*, XLV, 1931.

Daniel, G., *The Megalith Builders of Western Europe*, 1958.

Dillon, M. (Edit.), *Early Irish Society*, 1954.

Dillon, M., and Chadwick, N., *The Celtic Realms*, 1967.

Evans, A., *The Palace of Minos*, 1921.

Evans, E., *Prehistoric and Early Christian Ireland*, 1966.

Giot, P. R., *Brittany*, 1960.

Grinsell, L. V., *Dorset Barrows*, 1959.

Grinsell, L. V., *Victoria County History of Wiltshire*, 1957.

Hencken, H., *Indo-European Languages and Archaeology*, 1955.

Jones, G., and Jones, T. (Trans.), *The Mabinogion*, 1963.

Mongait, A. L., *Archaeology in the U.S.S.R.*, 1961.

Murphy, G., *Saga and Myth in Ancient Ireland*, 1961.

O'Kelly, M. J., 'An Early Bronze Age Ring-fort at Carrigillihy, Co. Cork', *Journal of the Cork Historical and Archaeological Society*, LVI, 1951.

O'Rahilly, T. F., *Early Irish History and Mythology*, 1946.
Ó Ríordáin, S. P., 'Excavations at Cush, Co. Limerick', *Proceedings of the Royal Irish Academy*, 45, 1940.
Ó Ríordáin, S. P., *Antiquities of the Irish Countryside*, 1953.
Ó Ríordáin, S. P., *Tara: The Monuments on the Hill*, 1965.
Ó Ríordáin, S. P., and Hartnett, P. J., 'The Excavation of Ballycatteen Fort, Co. Cork', *Proceedings of the Royal Irish Academy*, 49, 1943.
Piggott, S., 'The Early Bronze Age in Wessex', *Proceedings of the Prehistoric Society*, IV, 1938.
Piggott, S., 'Timber Circles: a Re-examination', *Archaeological Journal*, XCVI, 1940.
Piggott, S., *The West Kennet Long Barrow: Excavations 1955–56*, 1962.
Piggott, S. and C. M., 'Excavations of Barrows on Crichel and Launceston Downs, Dorset', *Archaeologia*, XC, 1944.
Raftery, J. (Edit.), *The Celts*, 1964.
Raftery, J., *Prehistoric Ireland*, 1951.
Rahtz, P. A., 'Farncombe Down Barrow, Berkshire', *Berkshire Archaeological Journal*, 60, 1962.
Rivet, A. L. F. (Edit.), *The Iron Age in Northern Britain*, 1966.
St. George Gray, H., interim reports on the excavations at Maumbury Rings, *Proceedings of the Dorset Field Club*, 29, 30, 31, 34, 35.
Schliemann, H., *Mycenae and Tiryns*, 1878.
Stone, J. F. S., and Thomas, L. C., 'The Use and Distribution of Faience in the Ancient East and Prehistoric Europe', *Proceedings of the Prehistoric Society*, XXII, 1956.
Thomas, H. H., 'The Source of the Stones of Stonehenge', *Antiquaries Journal*, III, 1923.
Tylecote, R. F., *Metallurgy in Archaeology*, 1962.
Wright, E. V., and Churchill, D. M., 'The Boats from North Ferriby, Yorkshire, England', *Proceedings of the Prehistoric Society*, XXXI, 1965.

Index

Index

Achilles, 17, 22–26, 86
Aegean civilisations, 47, 49, 50, 72, 120, 122
Agamemnon, 8, 17, 18, 23, 71, 72, 88, 106
Ancient Greek foot, 133–4
Aphrodite and Adonis, 41, 52, 92
Apollo, 45, 85, 91, 131
Arminghall, 152, 155, 161
Artemis, 53
Aryans, 20, 84, 93, 115
Ashbee, Paul, 2, 29, 30, 35, 65, 144
Atkinson, R. J. C., 2, 4, 7, 14, 15, 20, 31, 32, 41, 42, 45, 51, 97, 111, 113, 130–2, 135, 136
Avebury, 1, 7, 36–41, 51, 57, 62, 102, 103, 159

Beaker Cultures, 39, 40, 43, 55, 57, 58, 61, 131, 142, 154
Bersu, G., 98
Bibby, G., 47, 121
Boles Barrow, 7
Briciu's Feast, 79, 97
Bristol Avon, 7
Bristol Channel, 7, 50, 106, 129
Brittany, 7, 15, 51, 61, 63, 67, 68, 125, 158
brochs, 74–75
Bush Barrow, 12, 23, 29, 59, 60, 61, 64, 120, 152, 156

Carnac, 68
Case, H., 140–1, 144, 147, 154
Cattle Raid of Cooley, 25, 88–89, 93, 158
Caucasus Mountains, 20, 23, 115, 117
Chadwick, J., 52, 112
Champion's Portion, 78, 87, 91, 99
Childe, V. Gordon, 141, 144
Clandon Barrow, 59, 64, 67, 69, 152, 156
Clickhimin, 2, 74–81, 90, 91, 95, 100, 135, 144, 145, 147, 148, 149, 153, 154, 156, 157, 161, 162, 165, 166
Colt Hoare, R., 58, 59, 102, 146
Conall Cernach, 77, 78, 86, 87
Conchobar, King, 78, 80, 86, 87, 89, 90, 103
Connaught, 25, 77, 78, 88, 89
Corded-Ware-Battle-axe Cultures, 21, 26, 57, 116, 117
crescentic necklaces, 120
Crete, 7, 13, 32, 45–49, 51, 53, 70, 108, 114, 120
Crichel Down barrows, 152
Cu Chulainn, 21, 24, 25, 26, 77, 79, 86–92, 107
Cunnington, M. E., 34, 146, 152
Cunnington, William, 58
Cush, Co. Limerick, 146, 148
Cyclopes, 84–86

Dagda, the, 83, 84
Daniel, Glyn, 49, 50, 51, 119, 133
Delphi, 45, 52, 85, 91
Devizes Museum, 59
Diarmaid and Grainne, 92
Dorchester, 1, 62–67, 69, 103, 106, 156, 163, 164
Dorset Cursus, 67, 68
druids, 82, 83, 95, 136, 137, 159
Durrington Walls, 28, 29, 35, 98

Egypt, 14, 46, 124
Emain Macha, 77, 86, 90, 91, 149, 153
Evans, Arthur, 46, 70, 112

faience beads, 12, 14–15, 40, 60, 92, 93, 100, 107, 119
Finley, M. I., 159
Fomoire, 84–86

Golden Barrow, 59
gold, bronze, amber in Wessex, 12, 59–61, 63, 64, 105, 163
Golden Fleece, 6, 15, 17
Graves, Robert, 41, 45
Great Barrow, 60
Great Cursus, 29, 64, 98

Grinsell, L. V., 62, 141

Hades, 22, 92
Hamilton, J. R. C., 2, 74–81, 90, 98, 136, 137, 145, 161
Hawkins, Gerald S., 130–3
henges, 30, 35, 56, 140
Herodotus, 122–4
Highworth Circles, 153–4
Hittites, 20, 108, 115, 117
Homer, 1, 14, 15, 21–23, 66, 70, 71, 72, 82, 95, 122, 147
Hoyle, Fred, 130–1

Icknield Way, 44, 102, 105, 107
Iliad, 1, 3, 8, 17, 21–23, 24, 66, 71, 72, 88, 96, 117, 158
India, 17, 18, 19, 20, 25, 83, 86, 93, 114, 116
Indo-European attributes, 20–26, 32, 33, 41, 45, 52, 53, 85, 107, 110–18, 159, 164
Indra, 18, 19, 21, 24

Jackson, K. H., 24–25, 79
Jason, 6, 8, 14–15, 158

Kimmeridge shale, 63, 64, 65, 105, 121
Knossos, 46, 120

Lambourn Seven Barrows, 1, 62, 65, 69, 103–5, 142, 156, 163
Linear B script, 16, 52, 67, 90, 112, 114
Little Woodbury, 75, 80
Lleu Llaw, 18, 23
Los Millares, 47–50
Lug, 83, 84, 85, 86, 88, 162

Macha, 44, 90
Maiden Castle, 63, 64, 154
Manton Barrow, 60
Maumbury Rings, 65
Medb, Queen, 24, 78, 88
Megalithic art, 50
Menelaus, 106, 107, 129
Morrigan, the, 84, 89, 103
Mound of the Hostages, 49, 92, 96, 99
Mycenae, 7, 10, 23, 52, 58, 61, 64, 67, 70–73, 74, 86, 91, 108, 158, 159,

New Grange, 48–51, 57, 86
Newham, C. A., 133–4
Normanton Down, 12, 15, 29, 60, 64
N. Ferriby ships, 126–8, 155, 163, 164
Nuadu, King, 83, 84, 103

Oakley-Knowlton group, 1, 35, 53, 62, 65, 68–69, 106, 155, 163, 164
Odysseus, 16, 22, 84, 85, 106, 127, 162
Odyssey, 68, 71, 96, 121, 122
O'Kelly, M. J., 51, 97
Olympic Games, 69, 71
Olympus, Mount, 4
Ó Ríordáin, S. P., 49, 96

Patroclus, 22, 25
Phoenicians, 123–5, 129
Piggott, Stuart, 15, 35, 42, 51, 73, 116, 135, 145, 152, 158
Poor Lot barrows, 62, 63
Potnia, 52, 53, 156
Powell, T. G. E., 93, 159
Prescelly, Mount, 3–8, 33, 43, 111–14, 162
Pylos, 67, 112
Pytheas, 74, 125–6, 128

radio-carbon dating, 49, 73, 96, 116, 126, 141
Rath of the Synods, 99, 149
Rees, Alwyn and Brinley, 19, 25, 84
Ridge Way, 101–9
Rig Veda, 19, 20, 158
Rillaton Gold Cup, 119, 120, 158
ring-forts, 78, 97, 145–6, 148, 152, 154
Rinyo-Clacton Culture, 38–39, 56–57, 58, 148

Salisbury Avon, 7, 29, 35, 36, 111
Sanctuary, 42, 152, 161
Scandinavian rock-carvings, 32, 108, 128
Schliemann, H., 70–74, 161
Silbury Hill, 37, 40, 41
Silk Hill barrows, 36, 146
Skara Brae, 148, 149
Smith, I. F., 2, 36, 37, 38, 41, 57
Staigue Fort, 153
Stanton Harcourt, 140–3, 146, 147, 148, 152, 154, 155
Stone, J. F. S., 9, 15, 35, 57, 135
Stonehenge, 27–33, 130–9
  Altar Stone, 7, 31
  architecture, 13, 134–6
  astronomical theories, 130–4
  Aubrey Holes, 32, 34, 133, 135

bluestones, 3–8, 10, 33
carvings, 11, 27, 30–31, 43, 119, 120
linear measurements, 133
Y and Z Holes, 135, 137

Tara, 19, 28, 35, 49, 77, 80, 83, 86, 90, 92, 93, 95–100, 103, 146, 147, 149, 156, 165
Taylour, William, 119, 120
tholoi, 48
tin, 15, 46, 67, 125, 126
Trojan War, 22, 23, 52, 71, 85, 86
Troy, 17, 24, 26, 46, 71, 88, 129
Tuatha De Danann, 83–84, 138

Ulster, 21, 24, 25, 77, 79, 80, 86–90

Ventris, M., 16, 52, 73
Voyage of Argo, 14, 122

Wayland's Smithy, 51, 85, 103, 106
Wessex Culture, 13, 36, 43, 55, 58–61, 62, 64, 69, 100, 105, 106, 108, 129, 155, 156
West Harling, 145, 147
W. Kennet Long Barrow, 37, 42, 51, 56
White Horse, Uffington, 44, 103
Wicklow Mountains, 59
Windmill Hill Culture, 38, 39, 43, 56
Woodhenge, 1, 24, 29, 34, 64, 128, 135, 145–8, 152, 153, 154, 156, 161

Zeus, 3, 4, 8, 19, 20, 45, 52, 85, 86, 106

The Author

Patrick Crampton resides in Great Britain, and has been semi-professionally immersed in the archaeological studies of his country for many years, specializing in the British Late Neolithic and Early Bronze Age. His specialty within a specialty is the Salisbury Plain (Stonehenge), the Marlborough Downs (Avebury) and the Berkshire Downs. He is a member of the Council of the Berkshire Archaeological Society and of the Prehistoric Society.